MICHELANGELO
AND THE
SISTINE CHAPEL

'. . . come to the rescue / Of my dead painting now, and of my honour; / I'm not in a good place, and I'm no painter.' A sonnet by Michelangelo about the experience of painting the chapel ceiling, with self-portrait (see p.65 for a full translation).

MICHELANGELO
AND THE
SISTINE CHAPEL

Andrew Graham-Dixon

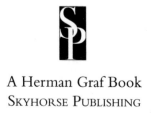

A Herman Graf Book
<small>Skyhorse Publishing</small>

759.5
GRA

Skyhorse Publishing books may be purchased in bulk at special discounts for sales
promotion, corporate gifts, fund-raising, or educational purposes. Special editions can
also be created to specifications. For details, contact the Special Sales Department,
Skyhorse Publishing, 555 Eighth Avenue, Suite 903, New York, NY 10018 or
info@skyhorsepublishing.com.

www.skyhorsepublishing.com

10 9 8 7 6 5 4 3 2 1

Library of Congress Cataloging-in-Publication Data

Graham-Dixon, Andrew.
Michelangelo and the Sistine Chapel / Andrew Graham-Dixon.
p. cm.
Includes bibliographical references and index.
ISBN 978-1-60239-368-4 (alk. paper)
1. Michelangelo Buonarroti, 1475-1564--Criticism and interpretation. 2. Mural
painting and decoration, Italian--Vatican City. 3. Mural painting and decoration,
Renaissance--Vatican City. 4. Bible. O. T.--Illustrations. 5. Cappella Sistina (Vatican
Palace, Vatican City) I. Michelangelo Buonarroti, 1475-1564. II. Title.
ND623.B9G66 2008
759.5--dc22
2008036409

Printed in the United States of America

Per Silvia

CONTENTS

The Genesis Cycle

1. The Separation of Light and Darkness
2. The Creation of the Sun, Moon and Plants
3. The Creation of Life in the Waters
4. The Creation of Adam
5. The Creation of Eve
6. The Temptation and Expulsion from Paradise
7. The Deluge
8. The Sacrifice of Noah
9. The Drunkenness of Noah

The Spandrel Paintings

10. David and Goliath
11. Judith and Holofernes
12. The Death of Haman
13. The Brazen Serpent

The Prophets and Sibyls

14. Libyan Sibyl
15. Daniel
16. Cumaean Sibyl
17. Isaiah
18. Delphic Sibyl
19. Zechariah
20. Joel
21. Erythraean Sibyl
22. Ezekiel
23. Persian Sibyl
24. Jeremiah
25. Jonah

Shaded areas: The Ancestors of Christ

26. **The Last Judgement**

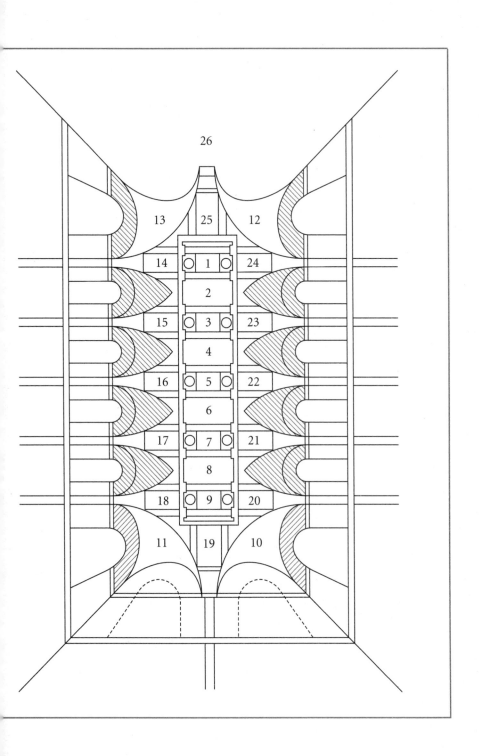

PREFACE

This book celebrates the five-hundredth anniversary of Michelangelo's commencement of work on the Sistine Chapel ceiling. It marks the cinquecentennial, as it were, of his very first brushstroke. My aim, in writing it, was to provide an informative and approachable introduction to one of the world's most rewarding works of art – and, in doing so, to fill a somewhat surprising gap.

While the existing literature on Michelangelo is vast, the sum total of commentary on the Sistine Chapel ceiling is smaller than might be supposed. It is certainly dwarfed by the literature on any single one of Shakespeare's major plays – *Hamlet*, or *King Lear*, for example. Furthermore, much of what has been written takes the form of specialised art historical enquiry.

Certain issues have tended to dominate scholarly discussion of the ceiling. In what order were the various pictures on the ceiling painted? To what extent was Michelangelo responsible for each particular image, and to what extent did he rely on the contributions of assistants? Was the iconography of the ceiling influenced by one or more of the theologians in the intimate circles of Michelangelo's patron, Pope Julius II, and can such influence – Joachite or perhaps Augustinian – be detected in the paintings? How did the architecture of the Sistine Chapel itself, and the sacred rituals performed there, shape Michelangelo's thinking? To what degree has his work survived the vicissitudes of time, and should the extensive late twentieth-century programme of restoration that so transformed the appearance of the paintings be applauded or condemned? Such questions have been extensively addressed, although often in rather piecemeal and partisan fashion, and mostly in learned articles published in art historical journals and periodicals. But there have been relatively few attempts to navigate between the various interpretations – to synthesise the existing knowledge and present it, in accessible form, to the general reader.

That is the primary purpose of this book, which is basically intended to be a user's guide to the Sistine Chapel ceiling. But I should say at the start that certain of the questions on which much ink has been spilled seem more interesting, to me, than others.

While various forms and figures in the minor parts of the ceiling were almost certainly carried out by the painter's assistants, it seems obvious, to my eye, that the vast majority of the work is Michelangelo's own. Such is the symphonic unity of the ceiling as a whole that it demand's to be regarded as, essentially, the creation of one man. Likewise, I consider much of the debate about the restoration of the ceiling to be fundamentally arid. The colours that emerged from beneath centuries of grime may have seemed disconcertingly sharp to those who had become accustomed to the layers of dirt with which time had smoked Michelangelo's paintings. But I believe that comparison of the ceiling with the works of Michelangelo's known admirers – the chromatically vivid *Deposition* of Pontormo in the small church of Santa Maria Felicità, in Florence, or Domenico Beccafumi's dazzlingly bright ceiling in Siena's Palazzo Communale – proves beyond doubt that the restoration did indeed allow us to see his frescoes in their true colours. To put the matter simply, it makes perfect sense that the Sistine Chapel ceiling as we now see it should have been a catalyst for the paintings of Michelangelo's followers; whereas the same thing could not have been said about the ceiling as it was before. The restoration was, in my opinion, both justified and brave. If only the authorities at the Louvre would be as bold in doing away with the murk of time that befogs Leonardo's *Mona Lisa*.

Leaving such questions aside, I have chosen to focus on what I regard as the essence of the Sistine Chapel ceiling – what Michelangelo meant by it, how its meanings unfold, the subtle ways through which he gave expressive life to its many interlinked compositions. Because it is impossible to understand or appreciate any work of art without an understanding of its context, I begin by telling the eventful story of the artist's own life, from birth to the moment when – reluctantly – he agreed to paint the ceiling for Julius II. I consider the nature of his early work and explore his unique, fiercely independent and often refractory personality, while also attempting to give the reader some sense of the world in which the painter lived and worked – its religion, its politics, its social conventions.

The heart of the book is my interpretation of the ceiling itself. This takes the form of an extended analysis of the work, both as a whole and also part by part, picture by picture. In addition, I briefly consider Michelangelo's subsequent contribution to the Sistine Chapel, *The Last Judgement*, and examine just a few of his later works in sculpture and drawing. This is because I believe those later works were themselves fruits of the same spiritual journey that produced the Sistine Chapel ceiling – and might therefore, among other things, be legitimately regarded as the older artist's reflections on his own younger self.

As a general rule, I have tried to give the greatest possible respect to Michelangelo's own attempts to influence posterity's perceptions of his life and work. This means that I often quote from the two early biographies of the artist, by his contemporaries Giorgio Vasari and Ascanio Condivi. It is my belief that these texts, although not written directly by Michelangelo himself, were so shaped by him that they reveal a great deal about his intentions, his beliefs, and his sense of his own significance. The problem is that they reveal those things often obliquely, through codes or parables or exaggerations. There are things in them, certainly, that are not literally true and may even be downright lies. But many of those falsehoods were, I believe, Michelangelo's way of expressing truths about himself for which he had no other language. More than any of the critical and art historical literature on the artist, Condivi and Vasari have been my touchstones.

I end by drawing the various threads of my argument about the ceiling together – and by attempting to spell out what I believe its central message to be. I do not expect everyone to agree with me. But I hope at least that the curious general reader who gets to the end of the book will feel better equipped to form their own conclusions.

I have been helped in numerous ways by numerous different people in the course of my work. I have benefited from conversations with Hugo Chapman and David Ekserdjian, experts both on Michelangelo's drawings (and much else besides). *Anche, grazie mille* to Giuliano Sacco, who kindly allowed me to print his fine Latin poem about Michelangelo. As ever, I feel guiltily indebted to my long-suffering family, who on this occasion put up both with my Michelangelo-induced moods and my Michelangelo-induced absences. Many thanks to the administration and staff of the Vatican Museums, who saved me countless hours by graciously allowing me to bypass the snaking line of pilgrims to the Sistine Chapel. Many thanks, as well, to Bea Hemming, Tomas Graves and the rest of the team at Weidenfeld & Nicolson for all their hard work and commitment in getting the book into shape and to press. I am also extremely grateful to my commissioning editor, Alan Samson, for persuading me to take the book on in the first place. But my greatest debt of all is to Silvia Sacco, my formidable researcher, without whom this book could certainly never have been written and to whom it is therefore dedicated.

INTRODUCTION

Michelangelo never wanted to paint the Sistine Chapel ceiling. He was daunted by the difficulty of the task and made it clear from the start that he resented the commission, which had been imposed upon him by the imperious and demanding 'warrior pope', Julius II. The artist persisted in the paranoid suspicion that the whole scheme had been cooked up by his enemies and rivals, to give him an opportunity to fail on the grandest scale and in the most embarrassing way. As they well knew, he was a sculptor, not a painter, and would be bound to make a fool of himself.

Besides, he had better things to do. The decoration of the ceiling of the chapel of the papal conclaves – all twelve thousand square feet of it – clearly struck Julius II as a fittingly grand scheme on which to employ the most prodigiously gifted artist of Renaissance Italy. But Michelangelo did not see it like that. For him it was a distraction from the yet more ambitious project, of a great monument sculpted from marble, to which he had already devoted years of his life, and on which his heart was set.

He reluctantly noted down the details of the contract for work on the ceiling in a memorandum written to himself – the earliest document confirming his acceptance of the commission – phrased with apparently heavy irony. 'Today, 10 May 1508, I, Michelangelo sculptor, have received from His Holiness our Lord Pope Julius II five hundred papal chamber ducats . . . on account of the painting of the vault of the chapel of Pope Sixtus for which I began work today under the conditions and agreements which appear in a document written by the Most Reverend Monsignor of Pavia and under my own hand.'[1] Michelangelo, sculptor, had reluctantly agreed to paint.

The 'Monsignor of Pavia' with whom he had made the agreement was Cardinal Alidosi, a favourite of Julius II who was soon to meet with a bloody death. The pope appointed him as legate of Bologna but Alidosi governed the city so ineffectively that he provoked a successful uprising against papal rule. Called upon to explain his failure, he made the mistake of heaping the blame on Duke Francesco della Rovere, the pope's nephew, and shortly afterwards the enraged duke stabbed Cardinal Alidosi to death in broad daylight on a street in Ravenna – a murder which went unpunished and largely unlamented.[2] Michelangelo was a superstitious man and this may have strengthened his gloomy conviction that the contract he had signed with Alidosi was an ill-omened deal. The murder took place in the summer of 1511, when after three years of back-breaking toil the artist was still wrestling with the decoration of the ceiling.

A year later, with the end at last in sight, he addressed a stoical letter from Rome to his home town of Florence, telling one of his brothers that the work was almost finished. He was plainly exhausted. But what shines through, despite the wearily laconic tone of the letter, is Michelangelo's belated, dawning sense of how much he had achieved, despite his own worst fears: 'I shall be home in September . . . I work harder than anyone who ever lived. I am not well and worn out with this stupendous labour and yet I am patient in order to achieve the desired end.'[3]

Posterity has rarely regretted Michelangelo's grudging acquiescence in taking on his 'stupendous labour', although there have been occasional dissenting voices. Barely ten years after the artist had finished his work, the newly elected, notoriously ascetic and – much to Rome's relief – short-lived Pope Hadrian VI is said to have turned a baleful eye up to the ceiling, and to have curtly dismissed it as 'a bathroom of nudes'.[4] The most prolific and influential art critic of nineteenth-century England, John Ruskin, was similarly disconcerted by the ceiling's many nude figures. He regarded it as a work of retrograde genius, which replaced the innocent piety of early Renaissance Christian art with the turbulent energies of a dangerous sensualism. Ruskin even went so far, in a lecture given in Oxford in 1871, to describe Michelangelo as 'the chief captain of evil' of the Italian Renaissance.

Despite such outbreaks of misplaced prudishness, there has otherwise been broad consensus about the quality and importance of Michelangelo's paintings for the Sistine Chapel. Collectively they represent one of the highest pinnacles of creative achievement – an equivalent, in the visual arts, to the poetry of Dante and Milton, or the music of Bach. The most fervent admirers of the fresco cycle go further, arguing that it is the single greatest work of painting in the entire history of Western civilisation.

That was certainly the opinion of Sir Joshua Reynolds, the founding president of the Royal Academy, who dedicated the last and most emotional of his *Discourses on Art* to the subject of Michelangelo, the only artist whom he considered to have been 'truly divine'. Speaking to his students for the final time, on 10 December 1788, Reynolds regretted that he had spent his life painting portraits and imagined what he might do if he were a student once more: 'were I now to begin the world again, I would tread in the steps of that great master: to kiss the hem of his garment, to catch the slightest of his perfections, would be glory enough for an ambitious man.'[5]

Michelangelo occasionally seems in danger of disappearing behind the myths that have circulated about him, the many stories about his superhuman abilities, his 'divine' nature and talents. What is sometimes forgotten is that most of the elements of Michelangelo's legend were in place while he was still alive. For example, Reynolds's reference to the artist's supposed divinity has its origins in a flattering pun on the two parts of the artist's name, composed by Michelangelo's contemporary, the poet Ludovico Ariosto – 'Michael, more than human, Angel divine'.[6] This was then turned into a commonplace by the artist's friend and biographer, Giorgio Vasari. Vasari used the phrase 'the divine Michelangelo' so frequently as to turn it into a kind of Homeric epithet.

Novels and plays have been written about Michelangelo. Films have sought to dramatise his volatile personality and to tell the story of a life that was, for sure, anything but ordinary.[7] Such attempts to reanimate the artist have for the most part whittled him down to the wooden caricature of a tortured genius. But however they may have distorted the man, the very existence of such productions says something important about the nature of his achievement, and the nature of his originality. Michelangelo was one of the first artists to call forth intense speculation about his own identity and motives. It is no accident that people have wanted to flesh him out in fictions. His art made them want to do that. Perhaps the single most radical and revolutionary aspect of his work – and this is particularly true of the paintings he created for the Sistine Chapel ceiling – was the fact that it so strongly insisted on, and inflamed, precisely that kind of curiosity.

It cannot be too strongly emphasised that almost every form and figure, almost every image among the myriad images with which Michelangelo spanned the vault of the chapel, is starkly unconventional. He was well aware of the solutions that had been found by earlier generations of artists, who had illustrated the same Old Testament stories that were prescribed as his subject matter. But he did his utmost to avoid repeating them. The paintings that he produced, ranging from *The Separation of Light and Darkness* to *The Creation of Adam*, from *The Deluge* and the other stories of Noah to the depictions of the prophets, are exhilaratingly varied and inventive. But they bear little resemblance to any pictures made before their time. Even at the halfway stage of their completion, when the artist's scaffolding was moved across the vault to reveal the work he had done so far, what most immediately struck those who thronged to see the pictures was their utter originality. They were instantly recognised as a 'new and wonderful manner of painting'.[8]

There was, in fact, a well-established Renaissance convention of eschewing convention – of creating works of art with the explicit intention of leaving previous works of art in the shade. That tradition was particularly strong in Florence, the town where Michelangelo spent his formative years and began his career as an artist. It was embodied in the works of the quadrumvirate of Florentine masters who had reinvented the languages of painting, architecture and sculpture during the first half of the fifteenth century: Brunelleschi, who had erected the great dome of the city's cathedral; Ghiberti, creator of the bronze reliefs that decorated the doors to the city's Baptistry, famously dubbed by Michelangelo himself 'the doors of paradise'; Masaccio, painter of the frescoes for the Brancacci Chapel in the church of the Carmine, where Michelangelo drew and studied in his youth; and

Donatello, the sculptor of the marble *St George* that stood guard over the city's grain store at Orsanmichele, and the creator of the figures of prophets and saints, whether of *St John the Baptist* or *Mary Magdalene*, carved with such subtle realism they seem instinct with thought and on the point of speech.

Of those figures, it seems likely that Donatello meant the most to Michelangelo. This was not only because Michelangelo, himself, wanted to be a sculptor. A pupil of Donatello's, Bertoldo di Giovanni, almost certainly gave Michelangelo his own first lessons in sculpting; and the young artist's earliest surviving work, *The Madonna of the Stairs*, is a bas-relief evidently inspired by the bas-reliefs of Donatello. It may well be that Michelangelo felt that there was a direct line of inheritance between them, although in temperament and approach the two artists could not have been more different.

The source of Donatello's power as an artist is the strength of his faculty of imaginative *projection*. He asks himself what a desert prophet such as St John in the wilderness might actually have looked like, emaciated and wild, and he carves what he sees in his mind's eye. He asks himself what it might look like when a woman such as the vengeful biblical heroine Judith cuts a man's head off, and he casts the image in bronze. His works are compelling but they compel no meaningful interest in *him* because in creating them – in giving them such a strong sense of life that they present the illusion of being not works of art but actual human beings – he has absented himself.

Michelangelo is not like that. His originality is of a different order, his creativity of a different nature. The images presented by his paintings for the Sistine Chapel ceiling are not the product of any great sense of human empathy. If anything, they suggest that Michelangelo had little interest in entering into and genuinely sympathising with the lives of other people – in the field of his art, at least. It is impossible to *believe* in Michelangelo's Adam, in Michelangelo's Noah, in Michelangelo's people fleeing from the deluge, in anything like the same way that it is possible to believe in Donatello's figure of a wild-eyed prophet known as *Zuccone* (literally, 'pumpkin face'). Michelangelo's figures are removed from reality in such a way that they appear almost as phantasms or ideas.

The whole Sistine Chapel ceiling easily assumes the appearance of a phantasmagoria, in which all the images are united by their nature as emanations of Michelangelo's own thought and sensibility – his own contemplation of the truths that might lie embedded in the mysterious and often inscrutable Old Testament stories which he had been called upon to illuminate. The fresco cycle as a whole radiates a powerful and sometimes oppressively strong sense of introspection. Looking at it feels almost nothing like looking at the real world. It feels, instead, like looking inside the mind of the man who created it.

Michelangelo was an accomplished poet as well as a visual artist. That fact contains within it a clue to the particular, unique qualities of his painting. To draw a literary analogy, Michelangelo does not tell a story in the prosaic, direct manner of Boccaccio but in the poetically allusive style of Dante – the one Italian writer, according to Michelangelo's biographer Ascanio Condivi, whom the artist 'has always studied'. Every pose, every gesture, in the Sistine Chapel ceiling is charged with the sense of deliberation, intensity and polyvalence that words and phrases acquire in great poetry. No element of Michelangelo's work is without significance, depth, implication, sometimes to the point where his language becomes so fraught with possibility, so compressed and allusive, that it cannot be pinned down to the expression of any single doctrine or idea.

In this sense his spirit of innovation as a painter might be compared to that of Shakespeare as a writer – who, in *Hamlet*, invented what Frank Kermode describes as 'a new rhetoric', so inward-looking and so rich in complexity that 'sometimes it takes the poet beyond the limits of reason and intelligibility'. Nothing means only one thing and everything has been subjected to the immense pressure of the artist's thought. This holds for the larger patterns of meaning that play across the surface of the Sistine Chapel ceiling's surface, connecting one picture with another; it prevails too at the minute level of the smallest detail, epitomised by the most famous detail of the ceiling's most famous image of all – that small area of painted plaster where the whirling energies of a multitude are suddenly stilled, crystallised, to the particulate density of two fingers pointing across a few inches of air.

In short, Michelangelo did not just invent a new kind of art, but a new idea of what art could be. He put his own sensibility, his own intellect, his own need and desire to fathom the mysteries of the Christian faith, centre stage. Before considering the ceiling's many layers of meaning – the principal concern of this book – it will be helpful to consider Michelangelo's personality, insofar as it can be understood, and to give some account of his life in the years leading up to its creation.

PART ONE

*Michelangelo Buonarroti
and His World*

Michelangelo knew how deeply implicated he was in his own art and how closely it expressed his own thoughts and feelings. He wanted other people to recognise this too, although he understood that they might not find it easy to do. The notion of self-expression implicit in his work was not familiar to his contemporaries. They had no language to bring to bear upon it. No conventions existed for the discussion of such a phenomenon. Largely in order to clarify the nature of his achievements, Michelangelo paid a great deal of attention to establishing the story of his life, as he wished it to be known.

First he gave considerable assistance to Giorgio Vasari, who in 1550 published the earliest full biography of Michelangelo, much of it evidently drawn from conversations with the artist. Vasari's text appeared in the first edition of his pioneering *Lives of the Painters, Sculptors and Architects*. It was subsequently revised and extended for the second edition of 1568, but because Michelangelo was less than completely satisfied with Vasari's work he had already, by then, taken the unprecedented step of encouraging another writer to compose another biography – one that would be more acceptable to him. The author was Ascanio Condivi. Had he never written his *Life of Michelangelo*, published in Rome in 1553, Condivi would not now be remembered. Little is known about him other than that he was, for a time, one of Michelangelo's pupils and that he went on to become a distinctly unsuccessful artist. He disappears from history some time around 1574, when he is said to have died while attempting to ford a stream.

Both of the early biographies are interestingly unreliable. They reveal a great deal about Michelangelo, but in no straightforward way, being written in a kind of code. Many of the stories that the authors recount, whether they tell of Michelangelo's youth and upbringing, his troubled but fruitful relationship with Pope Julius II, or his heroic endeavours in painting the ceiling, have the quality of parables or fables. They are stories with subtexts, stories that invite certain morals or messages to be drawn from the narratives that they present. Given that the source for nearly all of them was Michelangelo himself, it can be assumed that those morals and messages were ones that he himself intended readers to draw. In their oblique way they reveal all kinds of fascinating things about the artist, about how he thought of himself and how he wanted to be remembered. This is particularly true of Condivi's life, which was written in such close association with Michelangelo himself that it might plausibly be regarded as an autobiography written under dictation. It is a kind of work of art – Michelangelo's self-portrait, carved out in words rather than marble.

The two biographies occasionally disagree, both with each other and with the known historical facts, as they can be established from other documentary records of the time. But the lies that they perpetuate and the omissions of which they are guilty also shed light on Michelangelo's personality. A good example is the account given by Condivi of the artist's early training, which was clearly intended by Michelangelo as a corrective to the

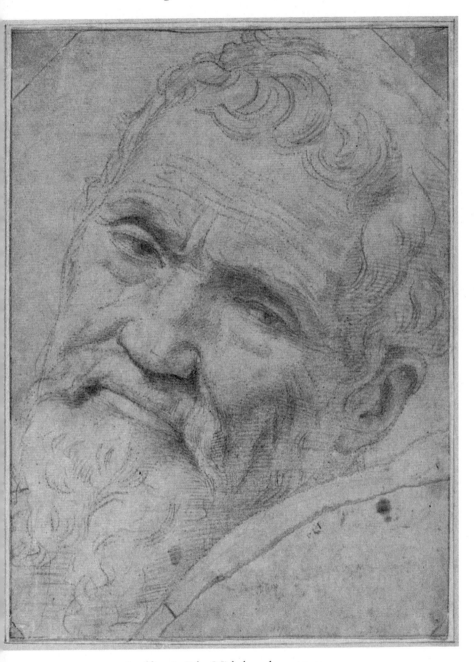

A self-portrait by Michelangelo, c. 1540s

account that had been given by Vasari in the first edition of the *Lives* of three years earlier.

Vasari had written that when Michelangelo was in his teens he was apprenticed to Domenico Ghirlandaio, one of the leading painters of late fifteenth-century Florence. Ghirlandaio was at that time working on his most celebrated work, a cycle of frescoes that can still be seen today, in the Tornabuoni Chapel in the church of Santa Maria Novella. This apparently harmless piece of information helps to explain how it was that Michelangelo, despite his insistence that he was essentially a sculptor rather than a painter, was able to tackle the painting of the Sistine Chapel ceiling with such vigour and assurance. He had been taught the principles and methods of painting in *buon fresco* in the workshop of one of its leading exponents.

Yet Condivi goes to great lengths to refute the idea that Ghirlandaio played any role whatsoever in Michelangelo's formation as an artist. In his telling of the story this was a myth put about by Ghirlandaio and his descendants, who were jealous of Michelangelo for having outshone them and told the lie so that they could bask in a little of his reflected glory. 'I wanted to mention this,' Condivi says, 'because I am told that Domenico's son attributes the excellence and *divinità* of Michelangelo to a great extent to his father's teaching, whereas he gave him no help whatever.'[1] For his part, Vasari was so enraged by the suggestion that he had got the story wrong that he marched off to Ghirlandaio's workshop and dug out the original copy of Michelangelo's contract of apprenticeship. In his second, revised life of the artist he quoted it chapter and verse with evident relish.

The truth is that Michelangelo was indeed taught the rudiments of painting in Ghirlandaio's workshop, but wanted to conceal the fact. A number of possible motives suggest themselves.

The idea that he was first and foremost a sculptor was always important to him. He told Condivi that sculpture was in his blood, relating that shortly after he was born, in 1475, he had been put out to a wet nurse in the little village of Settignano, near Arezzo in Tuscany. 'She was the daughter of a stonemason, and the wife of a stonemason. For this reason Michelangelo is wont to say, perhaps facetiously or perhaps even in earnest, that it is no wonder that the chisel has given him so much gratification.'

A more pressing need for the lie about his apprenticeship may have been Michelangelo's desire to preserve intact the aura of his own self-sufficiency. This pattern of suppression, revealing his desire to remove from the record any evidence that he was ever taught to paint or sculpt, was repeated when it came to the role played by Bertoldo di Giovanni in his early life. Whereas Vasari explicitly states that the artist was given lessons in sculpture by Bertoldo, in Condivi's adjusted version of the truth Bertoldo has simply been removed from the picture.

In fostering the myth of his own untutored genius, Michelangelo was not merely trying to put himself in a good light. He was trying to communicate something that he felt was morally if not literally true. Even though he had attended Ghirlandaio's workshop and even though Bertoldo had given him instruction, as far as Michelangelo was concerned, no one had the right to say they had taught him to be the artist that he became. He was different. He was unique.

Michelangelo told Giorgio Vasari a similar version of the story he related to Condivi about having been wet-nursed by a stonemason's daughter. Vasari, who was himself from Arezzo, near Settignano, where the wet nurse had lived, recalled Michelangelo's words: 'Giorgio, if I have anything of the good in my brain, it has come from my being born in the pure air of your country of

Arezzo, even as I sucked in with my nurse's milk the chisels and hammers with which I make my figures.'[2] However playfully expressed, the story implies that Michelangelo's conception of himself as an artist was tinged with uneasiness. He suggests not only that he has been marked out by fate, by God, to pursue a career in art. He also suggests an awareness that his destiny will not always be easy. Sucking in chisels and hammers – the artist makes his sense of vocation sound like something painfully ingested.

Little is known about Michelangelo's real mother, save that her name was Francesca and that she died when he was six years old. It was common practice at the time for families of some education and social pretension, such as his, to pass newborn babies to wet nurses for the first two years or so of their lives. So it can be assumed that Michelangelo had returned to the family home in Florence in about 1477 – only for his true mother to die just four years later. Mortality rates in fifteenth-century Italy were high, especially among young, child-bearing women. But the artist's early childhood was certainly traumatic, even by the standards of the time. Having been separated from his surrogate mother and lost his true mother in quick succession, he was soon to encounter difficulties in his relationship with his father.

Both Vasari and Condivi recount that Lodovico Buonarroti, recognising the boy's intelligence, sent Michelangelo to a grammar school in Florence run by a certain Maestro Francesco from Urbino. But as Condivi tells the story, 'nature and the heavens, which are difficult to withstand, were drawing him toward painting; so that he could not resist running off here and there to draw whenever he could steal some time and seeking the company of painters ... On this account he was resented and quite often beaten unreasonably by his father and his father's brothers who, being impervious to the excellence and nobility of art, detested it and felt that its appearance in their family was a disgrace.'[3]

There is probably an element of exaggeration here. Michelangelo was clearly a very well-educated man. Not only did he read Dante, he also wrote his own poetry, in fluent cursive handwriting. So it seems unlikely that he neglected his studies altogether. It is also clear that Michelangelo's father, Lodovico, eventually became sufficiently resigned to his son's inclinations to have him apprenticed to Domenico Ghirlandaio (although Condivi, of course, leaves that fact out). But there does nonetheless seem to have been a longstanding disapproval, within Michelangelo's family, of his choice of career.

The cause, as Condivi's choice of the word 'disgrace' suggests, was a form of snobbery. Although the status of artists had risen considerably in fifteenth-century Italy, in many quarters they were still commonly regarded as little better than glorified craftsmen. This seems to be have been so in Michelangelo's family. The Buonarroti were once-prosperous moneylenders – a traditional Florentine occupation – who had fallen on hard times. Michelangelo's grandfather, Lionardo, had squandered the family business, and by the time the artist was born the family estates had dwindled to no more than a little property in Florence and one small farm on a hillside in Settignano.

Yet still the Buonarroti persisted in thinking of themselves as rightful members of the leisured classes. They were landowners, albeit in a very small way, who preferred to subsist on the extremely poor revenues of their diminished estates rather than engage in anything as demeaning as manual labour. They might take on clerical duties in the counting houses of contemporaries such as the Strozzi, but working with their hands was out of the question.[4] The artist's father, Lodovico, must have hoped that the evidently gifted Michelangelo might one day restore the family fortunes.

But in choosing to become an artist – to be an apprentice, to work with his hands – there was in his father's eyes a clear danger that he might take the family even lower down the social scale than it had already fallen.

As things turned out, Michelangelo did more than restore the family fortunes. He became a rich man, frequenting the company of popes and cardinals. Throughout his meteoric rise he gave considerable financial support not only to his father but also to his varyingly feckless brothers, of whom he had four (one was a priest, who died young; the other three never amounted to much). Yet he always feared that his family would look down on him, despite his accomplishments.

More than three hundred of Michelangelo's letters to and from his father and siblings survive. They are overwhelmingly concerned with practicalities, mostly financial – the purchase of property, the banking of sums of money. Michelangelo's own letters testify to his sense of family duty and his considerable generosity, but they are constantly punctuated by complaints and lamentations. He lives wearied by gargantuan labours, he protests, again and again, and all for no thanks. A typical example is the letter he wrote to his father from Rome in October 1512, just after he had completed the Sistine Chapel ceiling, in which he concludes: 'all this I have done in order to help you, though you have never either recognised or believed it – God help you.'[5]

The most extraordinary thing about Michelangelo's letters to his family is the fact that he never once discusses his art with them in any moral or intellectual sense. It is ever-present in the background, as the cause of his exhaustion and source of whatever help he can give them. But that is all. Michelangelo may have felt that his family could never really understand who he was or what he was trying to accomplish. This may be another of the subtexts behind the story of the wet nurse and the miraculous capacities with which her milk had endowed the artist. Hellmut Wohl succinctly expresses this aspect of the story's secret meaning in his analysis of Condivi's *Life of Michelangelo*: 'As a sculptor, he implies, he was not the child of his father and mother, but of his wet nurse; he had been reborn, set apart from his natural heritage, and invested with a creative power that was his alone.'

All this may help to explain Michelangelo's extraordinary drive, his almost monastic dedication to work, his readiness to take on projects of such magnitude as to seem virtually unachievable – and, most of the time, actually to carry them off. He was motivated, in part, by a deep desire to prove his family wrong. It was an important part of his life's work to convince even the most sceptical that art could indeed be the noblest of professions.

★   ★   ★

Where did Michelangelo acquire his deep-seated belief in the nobility and intellectual seriousness of art? Largely from Florence and the traditions he encountered there. Brunelleschi, Masaccio, Donatello and Ghiberti, the founders of early Renaissance style, had not only furnished the city with copious examples of their ingenuity and talent. They had also effected the beginnings of a sea-change in attitudes to art and artists across the entire Italian peninsula. By the second half of the fifteenth century, the role of the artist itself had undergone a profound metamorphosis. The most gifted painters, sculptors and architects – men such as Piero della Francesca, who wrote a treatise on mathematics, or Leonardo da Vinci, who became expert in numerous branches of scientific knowledge – were no longer content to be regarded as mere craftsmen. They were intellectuals, possessors of special skills and forms of knowledge often so arcane they liked to refer to them as 'secrets' – men capable of mastering the complexities of human anatomy, or making the detailed calculations necessary to create the illusions of perspective.

The new skills and ambitions of artists were in turn recognised and encouraged by a new breed of patron. The princes who ruled the city-states of Renaissance Italy – the Sforza in Milan, the Gonzaga in Mantua, the Este in Ferrara – had themselves undergone a sea-change. Having emerged from the ranks of merchants and mercenaries, their horizons had been suddenly broadened by an intellectual revolution that took place in their midst. They too had learned to value different forms of learning, in particular to share that interest in the classical past proselytised by the men hired to educate them. Their teachers were drawn increasingly from the ranks of humanist scholars, followers of Petrarch, united by a fascination for what he had called 'the pure radiance of the past'. The princely patrons of Renaissance Italy themselves became intrigued by the past and consumed by the ambition to rival the glory of antiquity.

Michelangelo experienced this new world at first hand during his formative years, when he came into direct contact with the circle of the Medici, the principal family of Florence. At its head was Lorenzo de' Medici, otherwise known as Il Magnifico, 'The Magnificent One', who gave much encouragement to the artist in his early years. Vasari tells the story behind their first meeting, which took place when Michelangelo was no more than fifteen years old, in convincingly circumstantial detail:

> At that time the Magnificent Lorenzo de' Medici kept the sculptor Bertoldo in his garden on the Piazza San Marco, not so much as custodian or guardian of the many beautiful antiques that he had collected and gathered together at great expense in that place, as because, desiring very earnestly to create a school

of excellent painters and sculptors, he wished that these should have as their chief and guide the above-named Bertoldo, who was a disciple of Donato [Donatello] . Bertoldo, although he was so old that he was not able to work, was nevertheless a well-practised master and in much repute ... Now Lorenzo, who bore a very great love to painting and to sculpture, was grieved that there were not to be found in his time sculptors noble and famous enough to equal the many painters of the highest merit and reputation, and he determined, as I have said, to found a school. To this end he besought Domenico Ghirlandaio that, if he had among the young men in his workshop any that were inclined to sculpture, he might send them to his garden, where he wished to train and form them in such a manner as might do honour to himself, to Domenico, and to the whole city. Whereupon there were given to him by Domenico as the best of his young men, among others, Michelangelo and Francesco Granacci ...[6]

Some modern scholars have unaccountably chosen to regard Lorenzo's sculpture garden as a fiction. But it certainly existed. It contained an avenue of cypresses and a loggia, as well as Lorenzo's collection of classical statuary. Vasari goes so far as to call it an art academy, in which case it would have been one of the first such institutions, although his actual description makes it sound a little more informal than that – a place where young men could study sculpture in their own time and make their first attempts in the medium, sporadically supervised by Bertoldo, the ageing tutor-cum-custodian. Lorenzo the Magnificent had a habit of turning up unannounced to inspect the progress of his young protégés.[7] According to both of Michelangelo's biographers, he took to Michelangelo more or less instantly.

Condivi tells the story of how Michelangelo decided to make his own copy of one of Lorenzo's classical statues:

> One day, he was examining among these works the *Head of a Faun*, already old in appearance, with a long beard and laughing countenance, though the mouth, on account of its antiquity, could hardly be distinguished or recognised for what it was; and, as he liked it inordinately, he decided to copy it in marble ... He set about copying the *Faun* with such care and study that in a few days he perfected it, supplying from his imagination all that was lacking in the ancient work, that is, the open mouth as of a man laughing, so that the cavity of the mouth and all the teeth could be seen. In the midst of this, the Magnificent, coming to see what point his works had reached, found the boy engaged in polishing the head and, approaching quite near, he was much amazed, considering first the excellence of the work and then the boy's age; and, although he did praise the work, nonetheless he joked with him as with a child and said, 'Oh, you have made the *Faun* old and left him all his teeth. Don't you know that old men of that age are always missing a few?'[8]

As soon as Lorenzo had left, Michelangelo got to work on the statue, removing an upper tooth from its mouth and drilling a hole in the gum to make it look as though it had come out by the root:

> '... the following day he awaited the Magnificent with eager longing. When he had come and noted the boy's goodness and simplicity, he laughed at him very much; but then, when he weighed in his mind the perfection of the thing and the age of the boy, he, who was the father of *virtù*, resolved to help and

encourage such great genius and to take him into his household; and, learning from him whose son he was, he said: 'Inform your father that I would like to speak to him.'[9]

Michelangelo's father does not emerge with much credit from the rest of Condivi's account. When Lodovico hears that he has been summoned, he suspects that he is being manipulated by Michelangelo. He protests that he will never suffer his son to become a mere stonemason, and refuses to listen when it is explained to him 'how great a difference there was between a sculptor and a stonemason'. However, he cannot refuse to meet Lorenzo the Magnificent, who is so much his social superior. Lorenzo asks him 'whether he would be willing to let him have his son for his own', in exchange for which he promises to grant him 'the greatest favour in my power'. Lodovico agrees but, like some hapless character in a fairy story, immediately fails to take advantage of his fortunate situation. Offered, as if by magic, anything he might wish for, he asks for a minor job in the customs office. Lorenzo claps him on the shoulder and smiles at his naïveté, commenting, 'You will always be poor.'[10]

The contrast between Lodovico's lack of ambition and his son's strength of purpose could hardly be greater. Concealed within this parable of a father who foolishly fails to understand the nature of his son's genius, then even more foolishly fails to profit by it, lies a message from Michelangelo to his contemporaries. Lodovico, who cannot grasp the difference between a sculptor and a mere stonemason, represents all of those who would doubt the true dignity of the artist's vocation. His objections, rooted in snobbery, are made to seem all the more absurd by the fact that it is a member of the noble house of the Medici who refutes them.

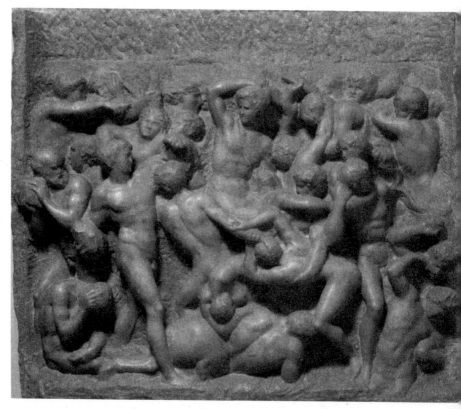

The Battle of the Centaurs

The moment when Lorenzo il Magnifico took him into his household was always regarded by Michelangelo as a milestone in his life. According to both Vasari and Condivi, Lorenzo treated the artist as if he were one of his own sons. Michelangelo ate at Lorenzo's table and benefited from conversations with the many leading humanist authors who were part of the Medici circle. He is said to have been inspired to create one of his earliest works, a bas-relief on the classical theme of *The Battle of the Centaurs* (above), by the poet Angelo Poliziano. The work in question, which was not a commission but was created for the artist's own satisfaction, remained in the hands of his heirs for centuries and can still be seen in the Casa Buonarroti in Florence. This study in writhing, intertwined human bodies is a testament to Michelangelo's extraordinary abilities with a chisel, at the age of just sixteen or seventeen. It is also evidence of his volatility of temperament and his deep sensuality.

It has often been asserted that the artist fell under the sway of Neo-Platonic philosophy while in the Medici household. But there is no strong evidence for this. There is no supposedly Neo-Platonic reference, in his work either as an artist or as a poet, that cannot be more straightforwardly explained as an expression of Christian belief. The most clearly identifiable legacies of his early exposure to humanist scholarship were a fascination with the art of antiquity and a strongly independent cast of mind – a determination to approach every subject that he drew, painted or sculpted as if he were the first artist ever to treat it.

There has been much speculation about which particular humanist texts Michelangelo might have read in his youth. Pico della Mirandola's *Oration on the Dignity of Man* has been cited so often, in relation to Michelangelo, as to suggest that it must have been a key influence on him, one of his intellectual touchstones. But there is no sign that he ever read it and no reason to think it ever mattered to him.

Humanist thought exerted its strongest influence on him through no particular, individual text, but through its radically new sense of what a text actually *is*. This amounted, also, to a whole new way of thinking. During the Middle Ages, classical texts ranging from the works of Cicero to those of Galen had been regarded as 'authorities', bundles of statements and beliefs hallowed by tradition and therefore to be taken on trust. The humanists revolutionised this attitude. They came to believe that every classical text was to be treated on its own merits, analysed on first principles, and evaluated accordingly. For Michelangelo's contemporary, the celebrated scholar Desiderio Erasmus, the project of re-reading the past became connected with the need for spiritual reform across all Christendom. For too long had Scripture been the property of the Church. For too long had theologians been allowed to barnacle the words of the Old and New Testaments with their own complex interpretations and exegeses. It was time to recover God's message in its purity – and to contemplate that message, as if for the first time, in a state of spiritual innocence and nakedness.

The same approach drives Michelangelo's particular form of originality, which is not to be explained as some mysterious emanation of genius but as a phenomenon deeply rooted in the intellectual history of his time. He has a strong and inalienable belief in his own right to read and interpret the Bible, to find and express the messages that he feels God has put there for the enlightenment of mankind. This is not to say that he is so arrogant as to set at naught the interpretations of the Church fathers, nor indeed of the theologians of his own time. But he does not take their authority at face value. He has the same independence of mind as a Christian humanist and it is this – just as much as his brilliance of imagination and abilities with a paintbrush – that makes the paintings of the Sistine Chapel ceiling so powerful and unique.

Lorenzo il Magnifico died two years after inviting Michelangelo to live with him. Within a few years the Medici had been expelled from the city, and the garden in which the artist created some of his earliest sculptures had been looted and destroyed. But Michelangelo had been spotted. In Lorenzo's informal academy, his horizons had been broadened far beyond the teachings of

Maestro Francesco of Urbino, whose school he had once sporadically attended. He had been taught the rudiments of sculpture.
He had shown such prodigious talent that it was already evident,
to anyone who had seen him work, that he was destined for great
things. He had taken the first steps along a path that would lead
him, circuitously, to the door of the Sistine Chapel.

★   ★   ★

After the death of Lorenzo il Magnifico, Vasari says, Michelangelo
returned to live in the house of his father, 'in infinite sorrow'.
Lorenzo's son, Piero de' Medici, showed a friendly interest in the
young sculptor. He sought his advice when purchasing works of
antique art. One winter, he is said to have asked Michelangelo to
create a statue from snow in the courtyard of the Medici palace. It
was 'very beautiful',[11] say both biographers, with tantalising vague-
ness. At around the same time, according to Vasari, he carved a
wooden crucifixion for the church of Santo Spirito, 'to please the
Prior, who placed rooms at his disposal, in which he was constantly
flaying dead bodies, in order to study the secrets of anatomy'.[12]
Vasari adds that Piero 'honoured Michelangelo on account of his
talents in such a manner that his father, beginning to see that he was
esteemed among the great, clothed him much more honourably
than he had been wont to do'.[13] Condivi says the same, adding that
Lodovico 'was by this time more friendly to his son'.[14] The doubting
father had at last learned the error of his ways.

During his early career, Michelangelo was to be singled out by
one discerning patron after another until the pope himself, Julius
II, would take him for his own and monopolise all his efforts and
energies. The artist's many stories about his youth make it clear
that he saw the hand of fate behind this chain of worldly events.
Before he was ever chosen by the Medici, or the pope, he had been
chosen by God. It is important to recognise that Michelangelo did

not believe this in any metaphorical way. In his mind, it was actually true. He felt that he had been given his gifts by God, and charged with serving the purposes of divine will. This is why, when he painted the Sistine Chapel, he depicted the Old Testament prophets with such sympathy and such a strong sense of identification. He felt that he had been called, just as they had, to spread the word of God.

The artist's belief that God was actively present in his life is implicit in both biographies but particularly strong in Condivi's text. For example, when the author tells the tale of how the young Michelangelo escaped harm when the population of Florence rose up against the Medici, it is clearly a parable of supernatural intervention. Condivi relates that the artist was friends with a member of Piero's retinue, a musician named Cardiere. One day Cardiere confided to Michelangelo that he had been granted a vision: 'Lorenzo de' Medici had appeared to him with a black robe, all in rags over his nakedness, and had commanded him to tell his son that he would shortly be driven from his house, never to return again.'[15]

At this point in the story, the artist urges Cardiere to tell Piero himself about the ill-omened apparition. When Cardiere does so he is laughed down as a superstitious fool by Piero and his retinue. But Michelangelo, who trusts in the apparition of Lorenzo as surely as Hamlet trusts in the ghost of his father, flees Florence for the safety of Venice and then Bologna. Once there, he is given refuge in the house of Giovanni Francesco Aldovrandi, a prominent nobleman of the city who would later become a favourite of Pope Julius II.

Aldovrandi, like Lorenzo before him, instantly recognises the artist's intelligence and talent. Like Lorenzo he takes on the role of the true father, the noble father that Michelangelo's own nobility had deserved. 'He was delighted with his intelligence, and every evening he had him read from Dante or Petrarch and sometimes from Boccaccio, until he fell asleep.' This idyll is interrupted when Michelangelo learns that there has been a popular uprising in Florence. 'At this point,' says Condivi, 'the Medici family with all their followers, who had been driven out of Florence, came on to Bologna ... thus Cardiere's vision or diabolical delusion or divine prediction or powerful imagination, whatever it was, came true. This is truly remarkable and worth recording, and I have related it just as I heard it from Michelangelo himself.'[16]

Michelangelo stayed with Gianfrancesco Aldovrandi for little more than a year before returning to his native Florence. The city was by then in the throes of a great upheaval, having been whipped into a collective frenzy of penitence by the sermons of the hellfire Dominican preacher Girolamo Savonarola. Savonarola had been preaching in Florence, to increasing popular enthusiasm, since before the death of Lorenzo il Magnifico. His sermons had been instrumental in the uprising against the Medici that had been correctly predicted in the dark vision of Cardiere – indeed, the friar had created a climate of hysteria and spiritual emergency that made men prone to visions and hallucinations.

Savonarola identified the Rome of the Borgia pope, Alexander VI, with the forces of the anti-Christ. His doom-laden interpretation of St John the Divine's visions in the Book of Revelation had led him to believe that the start of the sixteenth century marked the beginning of the end of the world – the start of the Final Conflict between the forces of good and evil. His call for spiritual reform was coloured by a deep sense of eschatological urgency. If the people of the world did not repent, if the Church did not mend its ways, and immediately, it would be too late. 'I say to you the church of God must be renewed, and it will be soon.'[17] Savonarola's pious revolution was destined to be over-thrown, its leader burned at the stake. But his impact on Michel-angelo's thought should not be underestimated. Even in old age, the artist said that the memory of Savonarola's words remained vivid in his imagination.

Savonarola was removed from power partly at the instigation of the papacy. But although he was regarded as troublesome and dangerous, a threat both to the Church's temporal power and to its spiritual authority, many of his ideas were reflected within the Vatican itself. He is sometimes regarded as a freak of history, when he was really a larger-than-life incarnation of attitudes extremely common at the time. Many others shared his apocalyptic view of the world.

Astronomers and theologians, Savonarola's contemporaries, nervously scanned the skies for comets that might portend the Second Coming. Omens were found everywhere. Plagues, floods and other natural catastrophes were interpreted as eruptions of the wrath of God. It was even widely assumed that Columbus's discovery of a new world must have been a sign from above, indicating the imminence of Armageddon – a heaven-sent oppor-tunity for mass conversion of the heathen, and therefore God's way of swelling his Christian armies, even as the satanic forces of Islam gathered in the East.[18] Astrologers competed to put a precise date to the world's final day. Italy at the end of the fifteenth century was extremely susceptible to eschatological terrors. As the historian Damian Thompson notes, 'the conventional picture of Renaissance Italy, in which a cultivated elite turns away from superstition and towards the study of art, architecture, music and astronomy, is extremely selective. We do not see the prophets wandering through Florence and Rome proclaiming the end of an age; nor do we spot the figure of the anti-Christ lurking behind the doric columns of the *renovatio*.'[19] In the art of the young Michelangelo – with its 'elite' references to classical antiquity and its deep, countervailing Christian piety – these very different attitudes are uniquely combined.

The greatest projects of the so-called High Renaissance, including the creation and decoration of the Sistine Chapel itself, were themselves bound up with a strong sense of 'end time'. The renovation of Rome, the rebuilding of St Peter's, the fortification of the Vatican – in papal circles these schemes were conceived not just as assertions of power and authority but as ways of readying the Church for the imminent judgement of the Last Day. One of the principal theologians at the court of Michelangelo's greatest patron, Pope Julius II, was the vicar-general of the Augustinian order, Giles of Viterbo. Giles, who may also have sought to influence the iconography of Michelangelo's paintings for the Sistine Chapel, gave explicit expression to this Messianic strain of thought. In a sermon preached in Julius's presence in 1507 he portrayed the pope as a figure to be equated with Moses, Socrates and St Peter, one destined to play a great part in the unfolding of God's awesome plan: 'You, after more than 250 popes, after 1,500 years, after so many Christians and emperors and kings, you and you alone . . . will build the roof of the most Holy Temple so that it reaches heaven.'

The literal reference was to St Peter's, but Giles had a larger meaning in mind too. Julius II was to preside over the creation of that greater Church, all of Christian humanity, drawn by Rome's splendour, as by a beacon, to fight on the side of good against evil in fulfilment of St John the Divine's visions of the apocalypse.[20] The commission to paint the Sistine Chapel ceiling was accompanied by the same sense of spiritual urgency that had animated

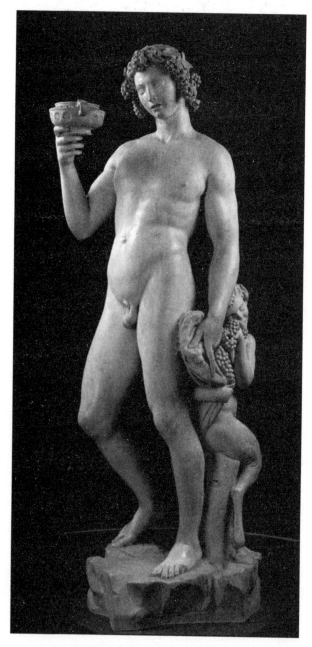

The Drunkenness of Bacchus

Savonarola, whose words had left such a strong impression on the young Michelangelo. The paintings for the ceiling would bear vivid traces of that apocalyptic anxiety.

★   ★   ★

Michelangelo left Florence in the summer of 1496, two years before Savonarola's downfall and execution. The cause of his departure was a fake. One of his works, a sleeping *Cupid*,[21] had been passed off as an antiquity by an unscrupulous Florentine dealer. A prominent collector in Rome, Cardinal Riario, had been duped into believing it was of ancient Roman provenance, and had paid the princely sum of two hundred ducats for it. After discovering that he had been the victim of a confidence trick, the cardinal had sent an envoy to Florence. The messenger was given two tasks: first, to track down the crooked dealer and get a refund; second, to find the artist responsible for such fine work and bring him to Rome. Michelangelo was twenty-two years old. His career was about to take off.

Riario was intrigued to meet the young prodigy. He even put him up in his own house for a year, according to the artist's biographers. Condivi says that although the cardinal gave Michelangelo no commissions, the artist 'did not lack a connoisseur who did make use of him; for Messer Jacopo Galli, a Roman gentleman of fine intellect, had him make in his house a marble *Bacchus* ten *palmi* high'.[22] The work in question, which unlike the faked *Cupid* still survives, is a life-size incarnation of the ancient god of wine, revelry and mystic orgies. Round-bellied and leering, the stone *Bacchus* (opposite) seems to stagger rather than walk, raising a glass as he teeters through space. Vasari wondered at the way in which Michelangelo had given the figure 'both the youthful slenderness of the male and the fullness and roundness of the female',[23] which has encouraged one or two subsequent commentators to find in it an early indication of the artist's presumed homosexuality.

★　　　★　　　★

There is no documentary proof that Michelangelo found men more attractive than women. He had close friendships with members of both sexes – most notably, in his later years, with Vittoria Colonna, whose piety and interest in spiritual reform he shared, as well as with a young Roman nobleman called Tommaso de' Cavalieri, to whom he dedicated some drawings and wrote letters that express his affections in the inscrutably formulaic language of courtly convention.

As he came towards the end of his biography of Michelangelo, Vasari felt the need to insist that the artist's love of the beautiful male form was totally innocent and pure. This suggests that there must have been rumours to the contrary. Such gossip was rife in the overwhelmingly male city of Rome. Michelangelo, who was both unmarried and extremely famous, was a natural target. Where does the truth lie?

On the evidence of his painting and sculpture, he was more strongly drawn to the representation of the male than the female form. But it would be unwise to draw firm inferences about his sexual orientation on the basis of that. He was fascinated by the art of classical antiquity, by sculptures such as the *Laocoön*, unearthed in Rome before his very eyes. The heroic male nude is essential to classical sculpture, the most fundamental element of its language. It became the basic unit of Michelangelo's expressive language as well, to the point where he could no more invent a composition without it than a writer could compose a sentence without words.

To complicate matters further, he wrote various love poems addressed to women when he was young. These include a comically coarse and erotically direct lyric, in three octave stanzas, in which he compares his beloved's body, part by part, to the produce of a farm. Her face is more beautiful than a turnip, her teeth whiter than a parsnip. Her eyes are the colour of treacle and her breasts like 'two ripe melons in a satchel'.[24] The poem is a farmyard parody of the courtly love tradition, a peasant's proclamation of desire for a dairymaid, so it should not be taken as a direct reflection of the artist's own feelings. But it shows that he was not only and exclusively interested in men.

The only really strong evidence about Michelangelo's sexuality indicates that he disapproved of sex altogether. The artist explicitly told his biographers that he preferred to have no intimate relationships at all, in order to preserve his energies for art. He repeated the sentiment in conversation with a friend: 'I already have a wife who is too much for me; one who keeps me unceasingly struggling on. It is my art, and my works are my children.'[25]

★   ★   ★

Michelangelo would spend almost his entire career creating art in the service of religion. Like a number of his other early works, the *Bacchus* is an exception. Perhaps that is why it seems to embody such a wild vitality, such an irrepressible sense of freedom. The strangely smiling figure, with distant unfocused eyes, is a dream of life as it might be lived without any sense of law or limit. The *Bacchus* exists outside the relentless arc of Christian time, outside its cycle of damnation and salvation. The figure is inscrutable, unjudgeable, unruly and alive. Michelangelo allows himself a reprieve from his own habits of spiritual solemnity – a sudden, drunken moment of release from the imperatives of his faith.

Shortly after creating the *Bacchus*, the artist carved the celebrated *Pietà* now in St Peter's (overleaf). He received the commission from a French cardinal who never lived to see the wonder

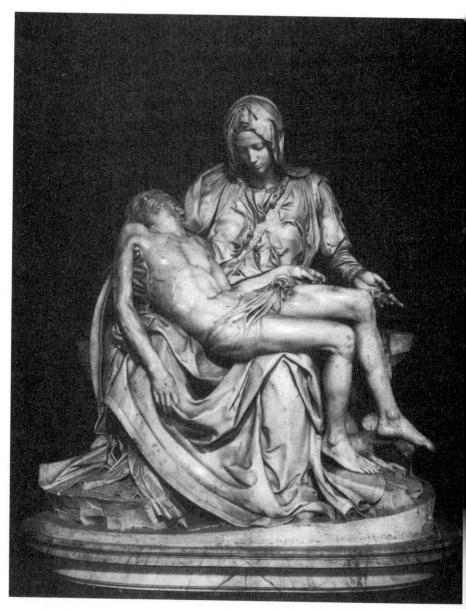

The Pietà *now in St Peter's*

he had paid for. The subject, unusual in Italian Renaissance art but common in the painting and sculpture of Northern Europe, is the Virgin Mary cradling the dead Christ on her lap. Michelangelo's Virgin is distant, so absorbed in her thoughts that she seems, paradoxically, to have less vitality than her dead son. She is withdrawn and remote, while his graceful form seems still to pulse, as if with the memory of life so recently stilled. She is swathed in stony draperies, while he is naked except for a loincloth. His body, carved with astonishing skill, has a deep pathos about it – the head that lolls back, the legs that dangle, but above all the limp right arm, gently squeezed at its juncture with Christ's torso by the pressure of the Virgin's hand, an arm rendered with such profound attention to each vein, every joint and bone and tendon, that it seems almost impossible that a human being armed only with hammer and chisel, let alone a young man of twenty-three years, could have created such a thing.

Vasari, searching for words to express the extent of his admiration for the work, remarks that 'it is a miracle that a stone without shape should be reduced to such perfection'. But the *Pietà* is unsettling too. Christ is as vulnerable, in his nakedness, as a baby. The draperies in Mary's lap suggest a shell or cave, a womb-like enclosure. She might almost be contemplating the terrible miracle of a full-grown but stillborn son. Artists had often depicted the Virgin as a young mother troubled by the foreknowledge of the agonies her baby will endure as an adult. Here Michelangelo telescopes time in the other direction, to suggest that in the moment of Christ's death Mary is remembering how she once cradled him as an infant.

Michelangelo had already been recognised by a few discerning connoisseurs as an artist of promise. But the *Pietà* made him famous. He was instantly acclaimed, not just as the most accomplished sculptor of his time but as a strange and truly marvellous phenomenon. How could an artist so extraordinarily young have produced a work of such astonishing complexity, such unprecedented truth to life? The myth of the 'divine' Michelangelo, sent down to earth by God himself, may have begun right at the start of his career.

The artist would himself grow to believe that he was an instrument of divine will. But he still wanted people to know that the *Pietà* had been shaped by his, by Michelangelo's, hands. The work became a popular attraction, drawing many of the pilgrims who flocked to Rome. Vasari tells the story of an outraged Michelangelo overhearing a man from Lombardy casually informing the rest of his group that the work had been sculpted by a certain sculptor named 'Giobbo', from Milan. According to Vasari, the artist crept into the chapel that housed the statue that same night, and sculpted his signature into the girdle that divides the Virgin's breasts. 'Michelangelo fecit' – Michelangelo made this. It was the first and last time that he ever deemed it necessary to sign his work.

★   ★   ★

In the spring of 1501, Michelangelo returned to Florence after five years in Rome. On his arrival, he agreed to sculpt a number of small statues for the tomb of Cardinal Piccolomini in Siena. He even signed a contract for the work, but soon asked for it to be set aside because he had a far more ambitious project in mind. In the workshops of the Duomo, Florence's cathedral, a great piece of marble had been gathering dust for nearly forty years. The block had been acquired in 1464 in the hope that it might be carved into a giant figure of a prophet for one of the cathedral's tribune buttresses. But the stone had defeated every sculptor's attempts to form it, and now it stood misshapen and abandoned.

According to Vasari, Michelangelo's friends in Florence had told him that Piero Soderini, the Gonfalonier of the city, was keen to see one more attempt made on the abortive block. So the artist went to investigate.

'Michelangelo measured it all anew,' writes Vasari, 'considering whether he might be able to carve a reasonable figure from that block by accommodating himself as to the attitude to the marble as it had been left all misshapen ... and he resolved to ask for it from Soderini and the wardens [of the cathedral], by whom it was granted to him as a thing of no value, they thinking that whatever he might make of it would be better than the state in which it was at that time.'[26] They had made a wise decision. Within three years Michelangelo had transformed the botched block of stone into a flawless and monumental figure of *David* (overleaf).

Vasari's own judgement of the work, pronounced some half-century after its creation, conveys some sense of the breathless amazement which '*il Gigante*' –'the Giant', as the sculpture was instantly nicknamed by the people of Florence – elicited from those who first saw it:

> He uncovered it, and it cannot be denied that this work has carried off the palm from all other statues, modern or ancient, Greek or Latin; and it may be said that neither the Marforio at Rome, nor the Tiber and the Nile of the Belvedere, nor the Giants of Monte Cavallo, are equal to it in any respect, with such just proportion, beauty and excellence did Michelangelo finish it ... And, of a truth, whoever has seen this work need not trouble to see any other work executed in sculpture, either in our own or other times, by no matter what craftsman.[27]

How did Michelangelo, still only in his mid-twenties, manage to create what Vasari rightly describes as one of the wonders of

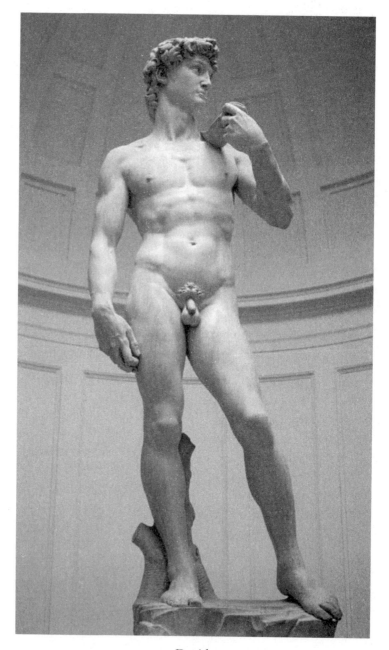

David

the world? This is one of the greatest mysteries concerning him. He had never been apprenticed to a sculptor. In fact there is nothing to suggest that he had ever received any extensive tuition in sculpture, aside from a few lessons from Bertoldo di Giovanni, the aged custodian of Lorenzo il Magnifico's sculpture garden. He had studied anatomy, but he was by no means alone in that – Leonardo da Vinci had studied anatomy more deeply than Michelangelo, yet he never showed anything like Michelangelo's abilities as a sculptor. Part of the answer would seem to be that Michelangelo was born with a rare and exceptionally strong form of spatial awareness, an ability to hold a particular three-dimensional form in his mind's eye, with total accuracy and for long periods of time. But it was also allied to an extraordinary manual dexterity, an instinctive ability to shape with his hands the images in his mind.

Vasari says that before making the *David*, Michelangelo made a model for it in wax. It was in the transition from that model to the finished work that he displayed his unique talents. One problem was that of scale, of translating the small image of the model into the gigantic size of the great block. The other and yet more difficult problem was to recreate an image formed by one process, but using a totally different technique. When Michelangelo made his model he was using an additive method, making a form by adding wax to wax, shaping and kneading it until he had what he wanted. When he made the *David* itself, he had to do the opposite. To carve is to remove, to chip away, to make a form by many acts of reduction. Most sculptors lose and find the desired form, lose and find it again, change it by a process of trial and error – all this as they go along. But for Michelangelo it seems that the form was *always there* for him in the marble, permanent and unchanging, as if it were simply waiting for him to reveal it.

Vasari says that he carved forms from stone as if he were pulling figures from water. This haunting metaphor sounds like one of the artist's own phrases. It may have been his attempt to describe, as best as he could, the mystery of his processes.

To express the matter simply, Michelangelo's brain was not the same as most people's brains. He might be compared to certain individuals who are gifted with seemingly inexplicable mathematical skills, such as the ability to solve the square root of an enormous number in a fraction of second. Some of Michelangelo's later architectural drawings, done at a time when he had been put in charge of the huge project of completing the new St Peter's, show that he could effortlessly manipulate particularly complex forms, like heavily moulded architraves, drawing them from all angles without any sign of calculation or workings-out – as if he had the equivalent of a modern computer-modelling program installed in his mind.

Certain drawings for the Sistine Chapel suggest that he made use of the same skill in creating his paintings for the vault. He would produce numerous, apparently disjointed, sketches and studies for a particular composition – an arm, a leg, a torso, modelled often from life, in widely differing conditions of light and shade. Then, in the act of painting, he would resolve this conflictingly lit jigsaw of shapes into a single unified whole. No other Renaissance painter drew with the same disregard for a consistent lighting scheme, and none worked with the same freedom from sketch to finished painting. Michelangelo could do this because of the skills he had shown as a sculptor – because of his unique ability to hold all the elements of a picture in his mind as if they were physical, three-dimensional presences. By the time he came to paint the image, it already existed so completely for him that he no longer needed to depend on his drawings. His

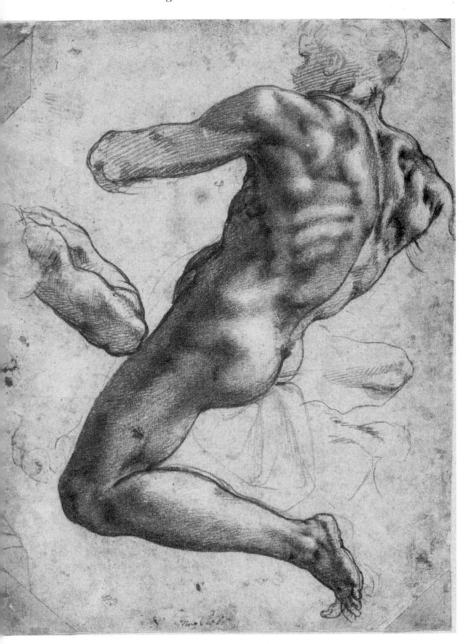

Study for the ceiling

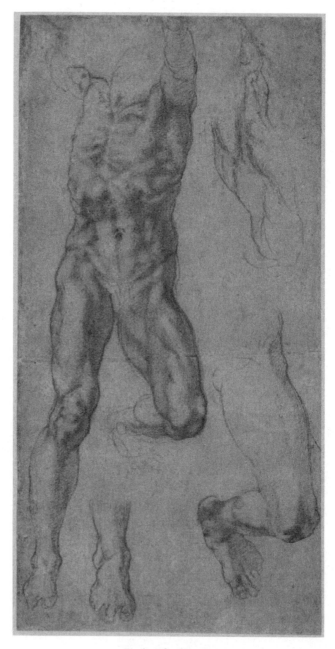

Studies for Haman

celebrated rival Raphael painted his frescoes on to meticulously squared-up drawings that had been transferred to the surface of the plaster. But towards the later stages of the Sistine ceiling, when he was at his most assured, Michelangelo was able to dispense with such laborious methods. He painted *The Separation of Light and Darkness*, for instance, freehand. Study of the plaster ground itself proves that he did it in a single session of no more than eight or nine hours.

⋆   ⋆   ⋆

Michelangelo was extremely busy during the years that followed his return to Florence in 1501. He carried out several other commissions for sculpture, as well as demonstrating his formidable abilities in the field of painting. He painted the so-called *Doni Tondo*, a roundel of the Holy Family now in the Uffizi Galleries, for a wealthy Florentine named Angelo Doni. The patron is said to have baulked at the price of seventy ducats, whereupon the proud and volatile artist promptly doubled it. (Picasso, who greatly admired Michelangelo, was fond of playing the same trick on recalcitrant would-be collectors of his own work.) During these years Michelangelo also created a vast cartoon, or preparatory sketch, for a painting of a famous Florentine military victory, *The Battle of Cascina*. This was intended to be one of a pair of monumental frescoes for the main hall of assembly in Florence's Palazzo della Signoria. The other painting, a depiction of *The Battle of Anghiari*, was commissioned from Leonardo da Vinci, but neither work got further than the drawing board.

Michelangelo's enormous drawing, which survives only in the form of a later copy, now at Holkham Hall (overleaf), showed a group of soldiers surprised by the call to battle as they were bathing in the Arno. With characteristic independence, he had treated the commission for a battle painting as the pretext for a complicated

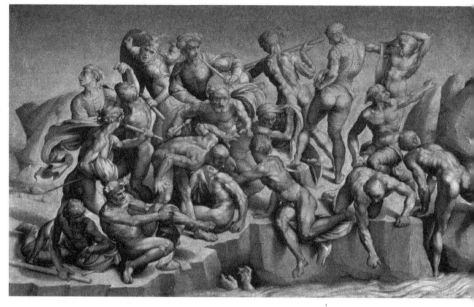

The Battle of Cascina, *after Michelangelo's drawing*

homage to the art of antiquity – a frieze-like composition thronged with naked male figures, each in a different pose, all suddenly energised by the urgency of a moment of crisis. The drawing was long preserved in Florence, where, according to Vasari, it became a kind of school for artists. Eventually it fell victim to its own fame: 'it was left with too little caution in the hands of the craftsmen, insomuch that . . . it was torn up and divided into many pieces.'

No such fate befell the statue of *David*. The sculpture of the young hero, sling at his shoulder, was regarded in Florence as an apt emblem of the city-state's own resolute determination to preserve its independence. Vasari indicates that the artist had always intended the work to be interpreted in that way. He also tells a story about the *David* that reflects on Michelangelo's ingenuity in getting his own way. It seems that when Michelangelo first unveiled the statue, Gonfaloniere Piero Soderini unwisely tempered his otherwise fulsome praise of the figure by commenting that its nose was too broad. The artist rushed to remedy the fault, or at least gave the appearance of doing so:

Michelangelo noticed that the Gonfalonier was beneath the Giant, and that his point of view prevented him from seeing it properly; but in order to satisfy him he climbed upon the staging, which was against the shoulders, and quickly took up a chisel in his left hand, with a little of the marble-dust that lay upon the planks of the staging, and then, beginning to strike lightly with the chisel, let fall the dust little by little, nor changed the nose a whit from what it was before. Then, looking down at the Gonfalonier, who stood watching him, he said, 'Look at it now.' 'I like it better,' said the Gonfalonier, 'you have given it life.' And so Michelangelo came down, laughing to himself at having satisfied that lord, for he had compassion on those who, in order to appear full of knowledge, talk about things of which they know nothing.[28]

Shortly after Michelangelo performed this cunning trick, a commission was formed to decide exactly where the marble giant should stand. Its members included two state heralds and a trumpeter as well as every artist of distinction in the city.[29] Leonardo da Vinci, Botticelli, Piero di Cosimo and the San Gallo brothers, among others, attended. The senior of the two heralds suggested putting the statue at the entrance to the Palazzo della Signoria, the civic heart of Florence. The site was already occupied by Donatello's bronze of *Judith and Holofernes*, another biblical allegory of the traditional Florentine disdain for despotism, which had been placed there as a warning to tyrants after Piero de'

Medici had been expelled from the city. But the herald argued that Donatello's work had brought bad luck to Florence: 'The *Judith* is a death-dealing sign,' he said, 'and it is not good for a woman to kill a man,' adding that things had gone 'from bad to worse' for the city since it was placed there. What better replacement could there be than the magnificent new sculpture of *David*? After long and tortuous deliberations, the herald's proposal was accepted.[30] At a stroke, Michelangelo's colossus had become the most prominent work of art in Florence. He had supplanted Donatello and secured his fame in the city where he had grown up. No wonder he believed that sculpture, not painting, was his true vocation.

★   ★   ★

The *David* was set in its place on 28 May 1504. Six months earlier, Cardinal Giuliano della Rovere had been elected Pope Julius II. Known to his contemporaries as '*Il Terribile*', 'The Terrible One', he was a fierce and warlike pope who spent much of his ten-year pontificate marching up and down the Italian peninsula at the head of his army. He wore a suit of silver armour and a silver beard to match. The beard, a novelty for a Renaissance pope, was no mark of piety. Julius II wore it in emulation of his ancient Roman namesake, Julius Caesar, who had once sworn that he would remain unshaven until he had avenged himself on the Gauls for massacring his legions. Julius II's beard was a pledge against his own numerous enemies – the French, the Bolognese, the Venetians, the Turks.[31]

'*Fuori i barbari!*' was the pope's warcry – 'Out with the barbarians!' He had been an implacable enemy of the Borgia pope, Alexander VI, and he was determined to recover the papal territories that had been lost to Borgia nepotism – to reclaim, in particular, the extensive lands in northern Italy that Alexander

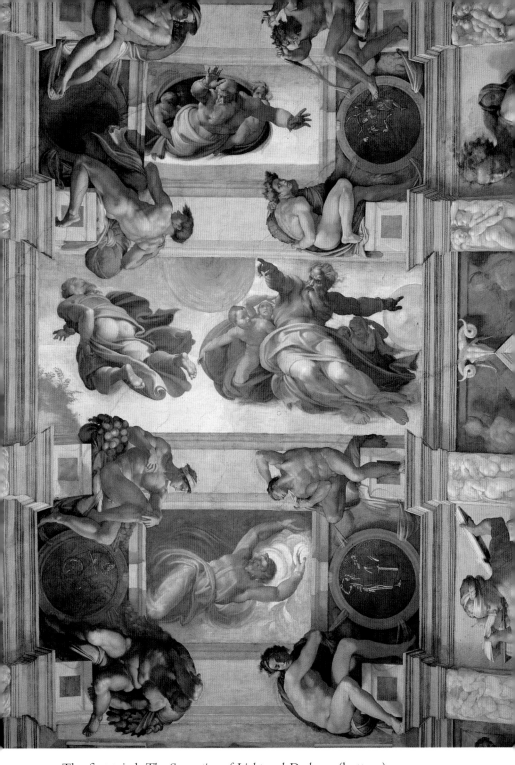

The first triad: *The Separation of Light and Darkness* (bottom),
The Creation of the Sun, Moon and Plants (centre and overleaf)
and *The Creation of Life in the Waters* (top)

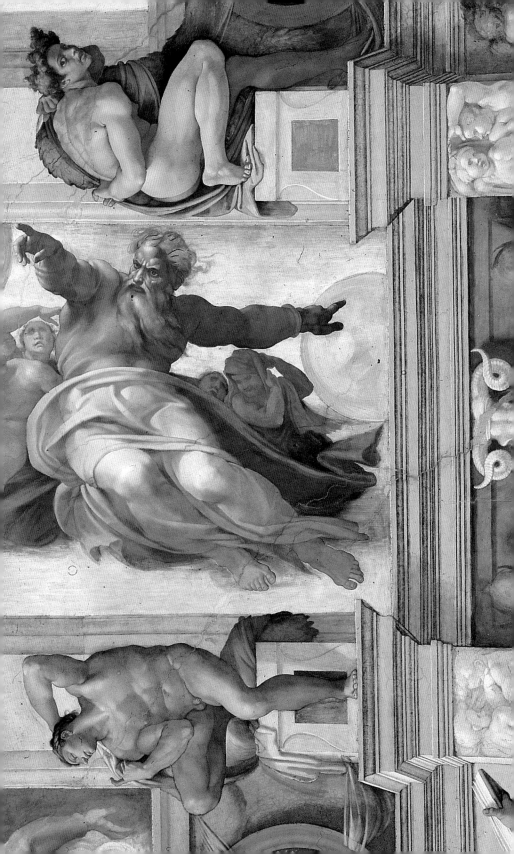

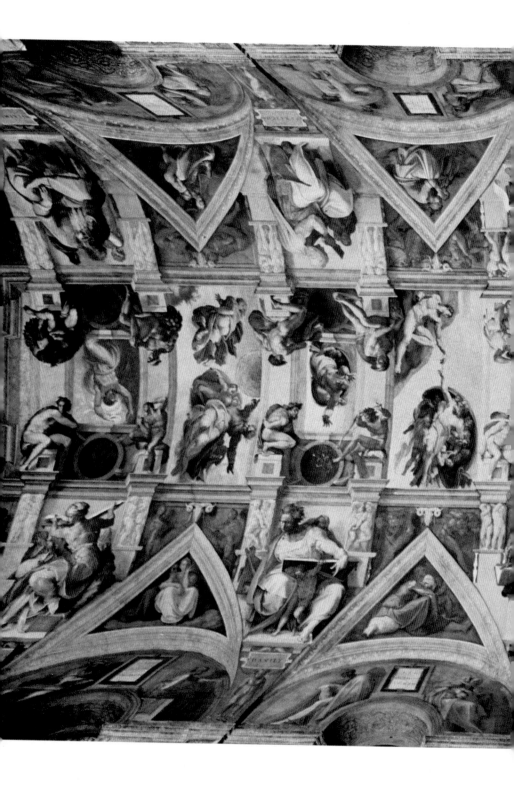

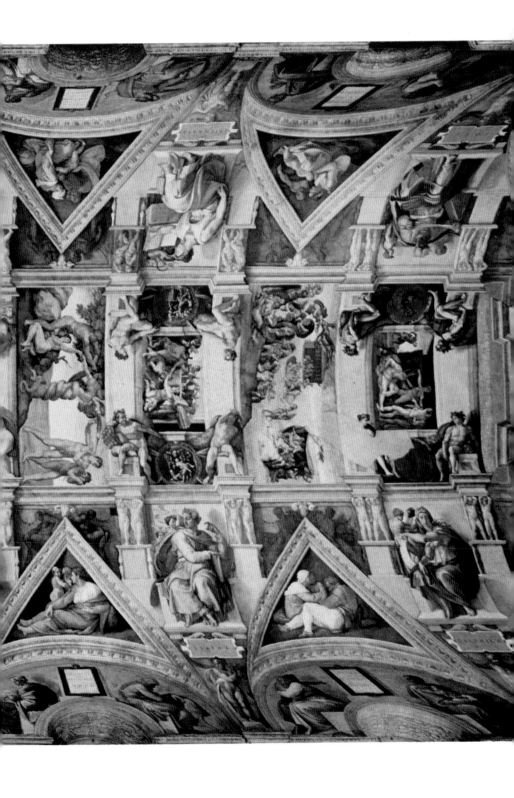

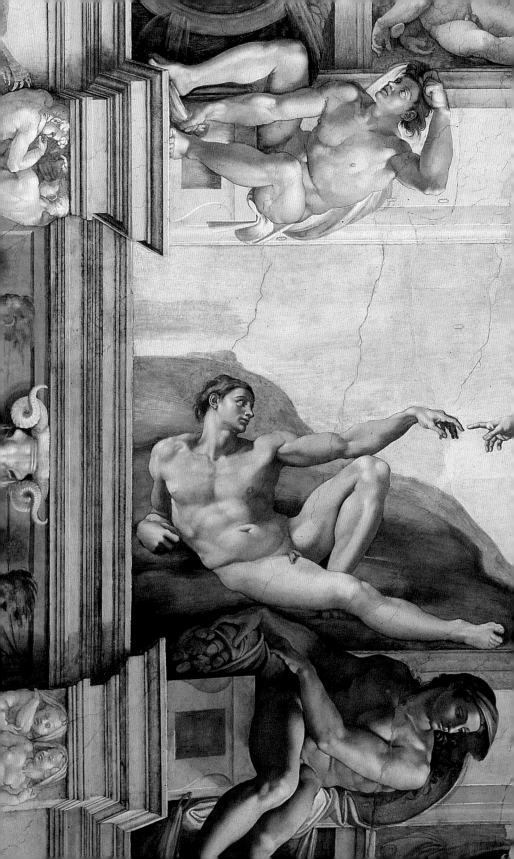

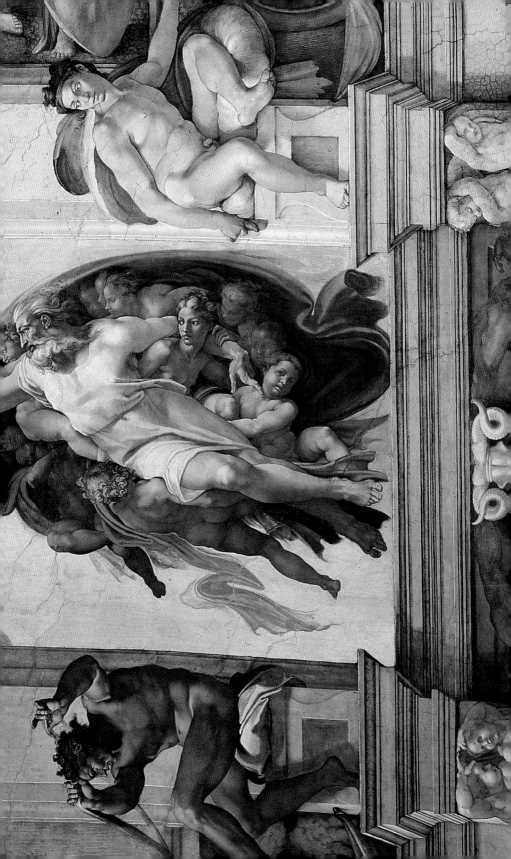

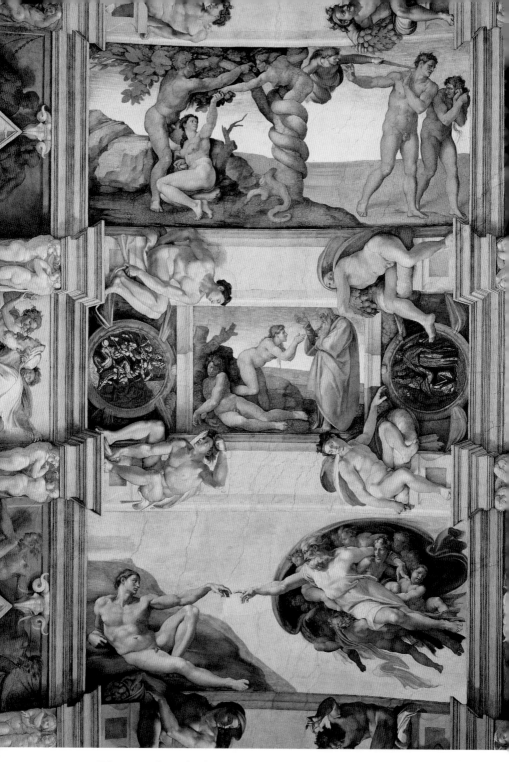

The central triad: *The Creation of Adam* (bottom and previous page),
The Creation of Eve (centre) and *The Temptation and Expulsion* (top)

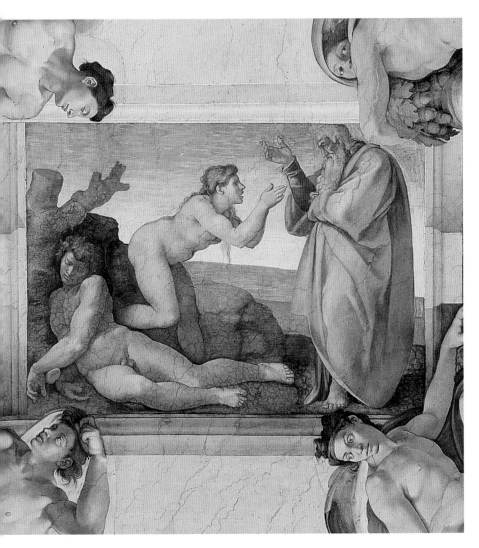

Above: *The Creation of Eve*

Overleaf: *The Temptation and Expulsion*

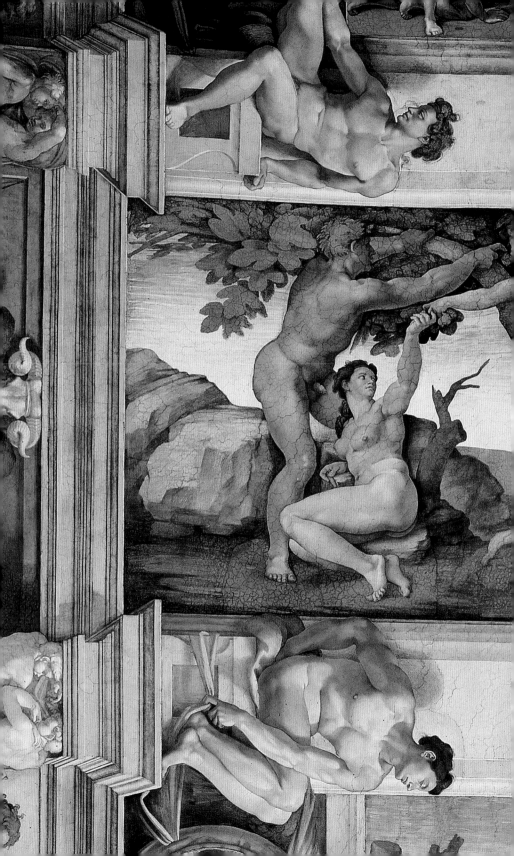

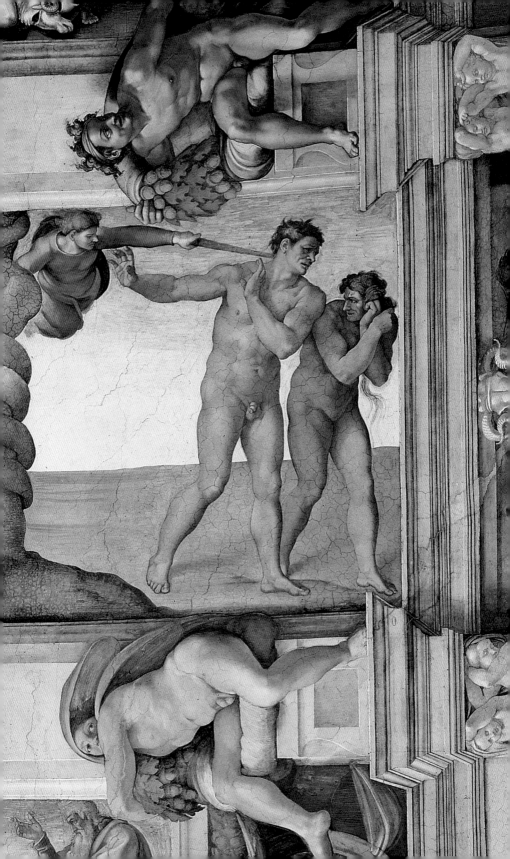

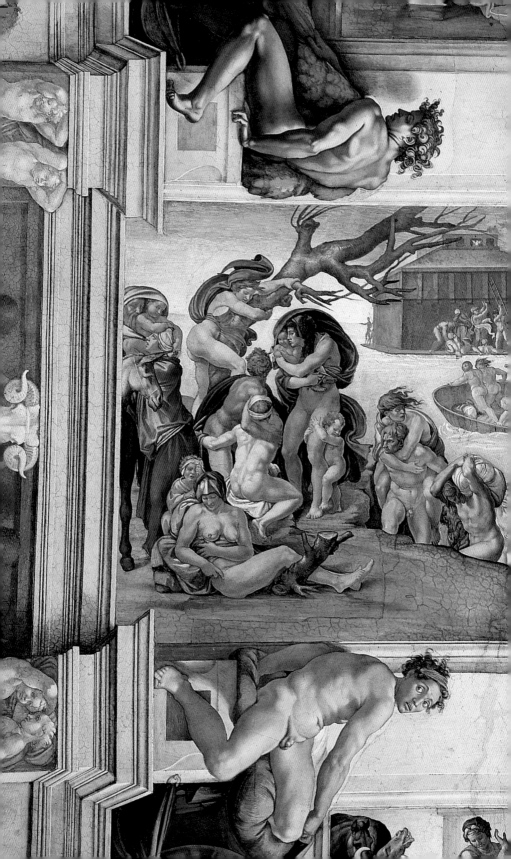

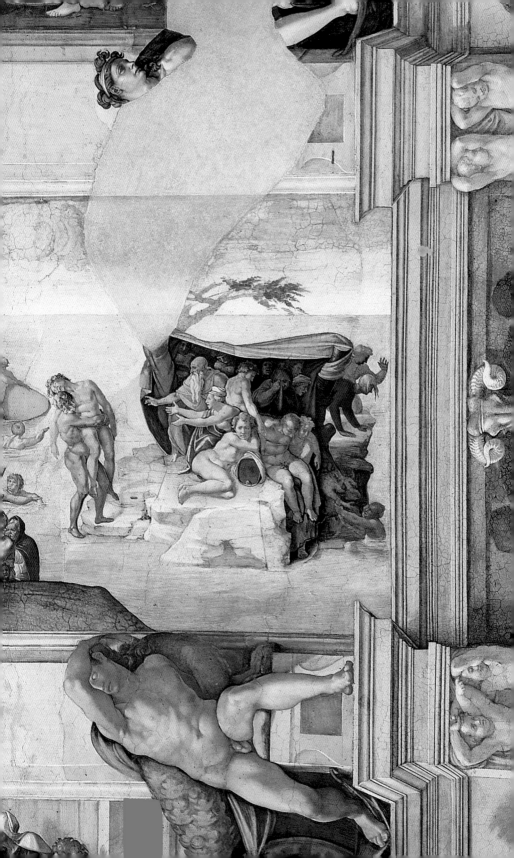

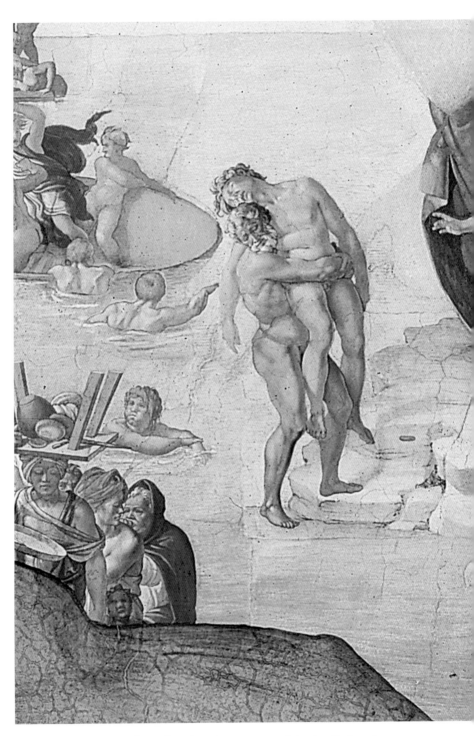

The Deluge (previous page and in detail above)

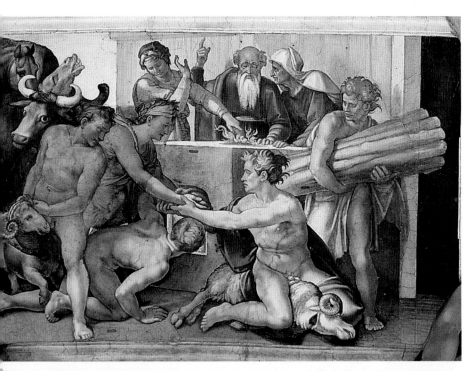

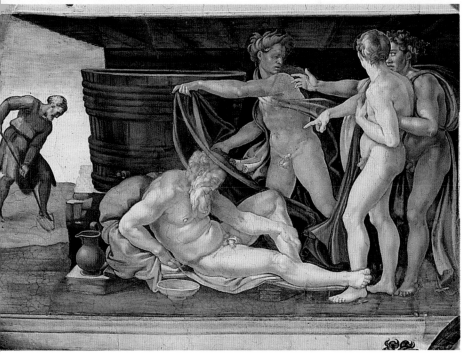

The Sacrifice of Noah (top) and *The Drunkenness of Noah* (below)

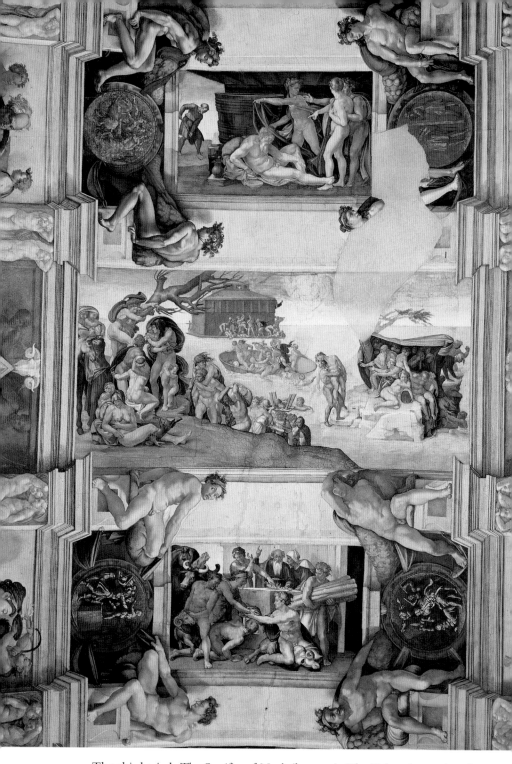

The third triad: *The Sacrifice of Noah* (bottom), *The Deluge* (centre) and
The Drunkenness of Noah (top)

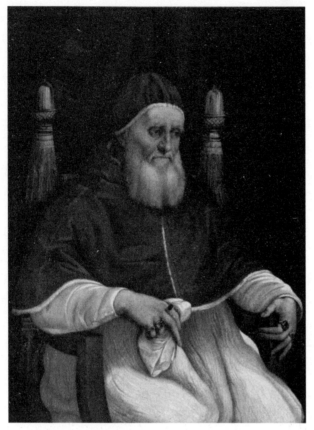

Pope Julius II by Raphael

VI's son, Cesare Borgia, had been allowed to carve into a state of his own. Julius II also fought to push back the Venetians, who had made steady incursions into the traditional papal territories of the Romagna. By the time of his death, in 1513, he had driven the French from Italy and brought Parma, Piacenza and Reggio Emilia into the papal states.

Despite his advanced age – he was sixty years old when he became pope – Julius II was a man of enormous energy. He was determined not only to redraw the map of political power in Italy, but also to transform the physical fabric of the Holy City. Despite its elevated status as the capital of western Christendom, early sixteenth-century Rome was little more than a series of linked villages clustered around the banks of the Tiber. The fabled seven hills of the city of the Caesars had become grassy wooded slopes, where sheep and cattle grazed amongst the overgrown ruins of temple, forum and amphitheatre. The gap-toothed hulk of the Colosseum towered over all, memorial to an empire long since extinct.

The city was derelict because of the decline that it had suffered during the Middle Ages. When Julius was elected to the papacy, Rome had only been home to the popes for a little more than eighty years. Martin V, whose election in 1417 had ended the Great Schism, had returned there in 1420. According to Platina, the fifteenth-century author of *The Lives of the Popes*, 'he found it so dilapidated that it bore hardly any resemblance to a city'.[32] Intervening popes had done what they could to build and rebuild the city's fortifications, streets, squares and fountains. Julius II's own uncle, Sixtus IV, whose pontificate began in 1471 and ended in 1484, had established the Vatican Library and rebuilt the old Palatine Chapel of Nicholas III – which henceforth, in Sixtus's memory, would be called the Sistine Chapel. Before that, a coherent vision of what the city might one day become had been set forth in a speech delivered in 1455 from his deathbed by Pope Nicholas V to his cardinals: 'to create solid and stable convictions in the minds of the uncultured masses, there must be something that appeals to the eye: a popular faith, sustained only in doctrines, will never be anything but feeble and vacillating. But if the authority of the Holy See were visibly displayed in majestic buildings, imperishable memorials and witnesses seemingly planted by the hand of God himself, belief would grow and strengthen like a tradition from one generation to another, and all the world would accept and revere it.'[33]

Julius II did more than any other Renaissance pope to turn this dream, a blueprint for the future magnificence of papal Rome, into reality. During his pontificate, the Vatican Palace was renovated and its new apartments decorated by Raphael with paintings that simultaneously celebrated the progress of human learning and the enlightened teachings of the Church. The Cortile del Belvedere was begun. New palaces were built, streets were widened and improved. Julius founded the Vatican museum and established Rome's most significant collection of the art of antiquity. He laid the foundation stone for the new St Peter's. He commanded his principal architect, Bramante, to improve access to the city for pilgrims by straightening the Via Lungara and building a parallel street on the other side of the Tiber – the Via Giulia, the longest straight road since Roman times.

He did all this, but at a cost. It was partly to raise the revenues for his many grand projects in Rome that Julius went to war so often. The territories he conquered became an important source of income, but the funds at his disposal could never match the scale of his ambition, so he resorted to other methods too. Simony and the traffic in indulgences – papally sanctioned pardons for sin, hawked across Europe by the agents of Rome – thrived under his pontificate. In the eyes of the pope and his advisers, the ends justified the means. Giles of Viterbo, favourite of Julius II and vicar-general of the Augustinian order, had a messianic vision of Rome becoming the new Jerusalem as the end of the world approached. Giles enthusiastically endorsed the sale of indulgences, never imagining the scale of the rebellion against the Church that this would soon inspire in Germany.[34] In 1517, only four years after Julius II's death, Martin Luther composed his ninety-five theses objecting to the sale of indulgences, precipitating the Reformation.

Julius II made some reforms to the monastic orders and dispatched missionaries to America, India, Ethiopia and the Congo. But he was destined to be remembered as a pope whose temporal policy had eclipsed his spiritual office. His pontificate culminated in a tragic paradox. In trying to realise the most grandiose dream of the post-Schismatic papacy, he had only helped to shatter it for ever. Although he had striven with all his might to consolidate the papal states and assert the immutable authority of the one true Church, his unscrupulous methods had fanned the embers of the Reformation that would sunder the Church and transform the very landscape of European Christianity into a war zone.[35]

In 1523, looking back at the pope's achievements from a post-Reformation perspective, Erasmus published a bitterly comic satire entitled *Julius Exclusus*. It tells the story of Julius meeting St Peter at the entrance to heaven and finding the gate locked against him. The pope protests, listing his military victories and citing the magnificence he has brought to Rome, but the saint remains adamant that he will not enter: 'You are a great builder: build yourself a new paradise.'[36]

★   ★   ★

From the moment of his election, it had been inevitable that the 'great builder' would call on the services of Michelangelo. Rome already contained an impressive advertisement of the artist's skills, in the shape of the *Pietà*, and stories about the marble colossus that he had created in Florence must soon have reached the pope's ears. Here, plainly, was an artist who could work on the scale demanded by Julius II's own enormous ambition.

The call came in the spring of 1505, when the pope summoned

Michelangelo to Rome. Well aware that papal patronage would open a new world of opportunities for him, the artist was happy to obey. According to Condivi, the pope spent several months wondering how to make use of Michelangelo's gifts before finally conceiving the idea of commissioning him to create his own tomb.

Michelangelo proposed a design of stunning scale and complexity, which Condivi describes in considerable detail: 'to give some idea of it, I will say briefly that this tomb was to have had four faces: two were to have been eighteen *braccia* long to serve as the sides, and two of twelve *braccia* as head and foot, so that it came to a square and a half. All around the exterior there were niches for statues . . .'[37] There were to be more than forty of these statues. Some were to depict the liberal arts as slaves, indicating that with the death of Julius painting, architecture and sculpture and 'all the artistic virtues' had been reduced to a state of feeble passivity. Others were to represent angels, both sad and happy, to lament the passing of Julius and to rejoice at his entry into heaven. There was even to be a second monument within the monument, a great tomb resembling a temple to house the sarcophagus containing the pope's remains.

So began what Michelangelo would, in later life, call 'the tragedy of the tomb'. It was a project on which he embarked with the highest hopes, but that was destined to be beset by a thousand interruptions and delays – one that would preoccupy him not only for years, but for decades of his life, and that would only be realised, belatedly and long after Julius II's death, in a much reduced form. It is hard, however, to share Michelangelo's belief that the failure of the project, in the form that he first planned it, amounted to a tragedy.

The Louvre in Paris contains certain figures of the slaves,

which the artist brought to varying states of completion, of an undeniable pathos and beauty. But the fact remains that the artist's initial proposal was a megalomaniac fantasy, an obscene monument to ego, pride and power. The oppressive object described by Condivi would have been no mere tomb, but a self-sufficient building, combining the functions of chapel and sarcophagus. It would have towered fifty feet in the air and would have occupied an area of eight hundred square feet. Its exterior would have been decorated with a multitude of niches, each containing a life-size statue, while, as Condivi says, four more statues, each one a giant, would have crowned its marble summit. One of these was actually carved by Michelangelo, the frowning figure of *Moses* that dominates the much reduced memorial that was eventually erected in the church of San Pietro in Vincoli. It is a statue that still evokes the chilling grandeur of Michelangelo's first idea for the tomb. Sigmund Freud was both fascinated and repelled by the work, and when he lived in Rome returned to it again and again, revelling masochistically in what he described as its grandiose repudiation of his merely mortal condition.

At a conservative estimate it would have taken Michelangelo between forty and fifty years to carve the monument's statues alone. Yet such was the pope's instant enthusiasm for the proposal that he allowed himself to be carried away by the artist's Herculean confidence in his own abilities. Michelangelo was dispatched straight away to Carrara, with an advance of a thousand papal ducats, to quarry the immense amount of marble required for the project. Condivi records that he stayed in the mountains for more than eight months, with only two helpers and a horse for company. He also tells a story that vividly conveys Michelangelo's frenetic state of mind at the time: 'One day while there, he was looking at the landscape, and he was seized with a wish to carve, out of a mountain overlooking the sea, a colossus which would be visible from afar to seafarers.'[38]

Once the quarrying was finished, Michelangelo returned to Rome, having arranged for the marble to be transported there by boat. It was unloaded at the port of Ripa Grande, then taken to the Piazza San Pietro, behind the church of Santa Caterina, near the artist's own lodgings. 'So great was the quantity of the blocks of marble,' says Condivi, 'that, when they were spread out in the piazza, they made other people marvel and rejoiced the pope, who conferred such great and boundless favours on Michelangelo that, when he had begun to work, he would go more and more often all the way to his house to see him, conversing with him there about the tomb and other matters no differently than he would have done with his own brother.'[39]

The brotherly relationship soon turned sour. In the spring of 1506 Julius II cancelled the commission for the tomb. His reasons for doing so are impossible to establish with absolute certainty. Perhaps he simply thought better of it. Even a man of his pride and ambition may have baulked, on sober reflection, at the idea of such an immense and permanent magnification of his own hubris. But other priorities had also come to the fore. He was involved in costly military campaigns and he had committed himself to a huge new architectural project, the rebuilding of St Peter's itself.

Michelangelo always believed that Bramante, Julius II's favourite architect, had played a devious part in the whole affair. In Michelangelo's version of the story, it was Bramante who had manipulated the pope into redirecting his energies towards the new St Peter's; and it was Bramante, acting out of naked self-interest, who had persuaded the pope that his money would be better spent on architecture than on the myriad sculptures of his multi-storied tomb. At his most paranoid, Michelangelo even believed that Bramante seeded the idea that he would be best employed painting the Sistine Chapel ceiling – part of a dastardly plot to make a fool of him by exposing his inadequacies as a painter of frescoes.

The truth is that Michelangelo himself may have been indirectly responsible for the pope's change of heart. The tomb that he had designed for Julius II was intended, from the outset, to be housed in the old basilica of St Peter's. But the plan for the monument was so grandiose that it could never have been accommodated within the relatively modest dimensions of that building. The pope may well have decided to enlarge St Peter's, in the first place, to make room for his own memorial – and then have grown so absorbed by Bramante's plan for the new building, and so aware of the enormous costs that it would involve, that he decided to shelve the tomb indefinitely.

Michelangelo only discovered what was going on by eavesdropping on one of the pope's conversations at mealtime. He told the story in a letter to his friend, the Florentine architect Giuliano da Sangallo. 'At table on Holy Saturday,' he wrote, 'I heard the pope say to a jeweller and to the master of ceremonies, to whom he was talking, that he did not wish to spend one *baiocco* more either on small stones or large ones.'[40] Michelangelo was alarmed at the remark, which he correctly took to imply that Julius II was no longer prepared to spend large sums on the marble for his tomb. He was also anxious because he had just parted with a considerable amount of his own money to pay off some of the workmen who had brought the marble from Carrara, in the expectation that he would be promptly reimbursed by the papal treasury. During the next few days, his worst fears were confirmed. Time after time he requested an audience with Julius II to settle the matter of his expenses, but on each occasion he was refused entry by the papal equerry. Again and again came the same answer: 'Forgive me, but I have orders not to admit you.' Finally, concluding that all was lost – that he would never get his money, that he had wasted eight months in the mountains of Carrara, that the project to which he had hoped to devote his life had been summarily terminated – the artist flew into a rage.

'Michelangelo,' writes Condivi,

to whom up to then no portiere had ever been drawn or door closed, seeing himself thus discarded, was angered by this turn of events and answered, 'And you may tell the pope from now on, if he wants me, he can look for me elsewhere.' So when he returned home he gave orders to two servants that he had that, when they had sold all the household furniture and collected the money, they were to follow him to Florence. He rode post and at two in the morning he reached Poggibonsi, a fortified town in the domain of Florence, some eighteen or twenty miles from the city. Here, being in a safe place, he alighted. Shortly afterwards, five couriers arrived from Julius, with orders to bring him back wherever they should find him. But they had come upon him in a place where they could do him no violence and, as Michelangelo threatened to have them killed if they attempted anything, they resorted to entreaties; these being of no avail, they did get him to agree that at least he would answer the pope's letter, which they had presented to him, and that he would write specifically that they had caught up with him in Florence, in order for the pope to understand that they had not been able to bring him back against his will. The tenor of the pope's letter was this: that, as soon as Michelangelo had seen the present letter, he was to return forthwith to Rome, under pain of his disfavour. To which Michelangelo answered briefly that he would never go back; that in return for his good and faithful service he did not deserve to be driven from the pope's presence like a villain; and that, since His Holiness no longer wished to pursue the tomb, he was freed from his obligation and did not wish to commit himself to anything else. When he had dated the letter as we said and dismissed the couriers, he went on to Florence ... [41]

The precise contents of the pope's letter are not known, but it may have contained the first of many demands that Michelangelo paint the Sistine Chapel ceiling. The subject had certainly been raised before Michelangelo stormed out of Rome – it is discussed in his correspondence of 1506[42] – but it may only have inflamed the artist's anger and sense of injustice. He had wanted to create a monument the like of which the world had never seen. As far as he was concerned, offering him the consolation prize of a mere fresco cycle was adding insult to injury.

★   ★   ★

Eventually, after months of sulking in his Florentine refuge, the artist was prevailed upon to make his peace with the pope. Julius II had suppressed the rebellious fiefdom of Bologna, bringing it once more under papal rule, and Michelangelo sought him out there. The pope rebuked the recalcitrant artist but then forgave him, sealing the new pact between them with a commission for a monumental sculpture in bronze. The work in question was to be a great statue of Julius II, three times the size of life. It was to be erected on the façade of the church of San Petronio, in the centre of Bologna, to remind the people of the city that their first loyalty should always be to the pope. Julius II specified that he should be shown holding a sword, rather than a book.

Michelangelo, who seems to have approved of the idea, replied by explaining his own conception of the statue's role: 'It is threatening this populace, Holy Father, if they are not prudent.'[43]

The commission turned out to be a poisoned chalice. The artist spent the best part of two years in Bologna, living four to a room with his assistants as he struggled with the difficulty of casting such a large work in bronze. After several abortive attempts, he succeeded in making the work, but within three years it was destroyed when the people of Bologna − brazenly defying the statue's warning to be 'prudent' − rebelled against the ineffective rule of the papal legate, Cardinal Alidosi. The bronze was melted down and turned into a cannon, 'La Giulia', mockingly named after the pope. After paying the wages of his assistants and covering the cost of materials, Michelangelo was left with the grand total of four and a half ducats for all his efforts.

In February 1508, with little to show for the last three years of his life, Michelangelo returned to Florence. He may have hoped that the pope would leave him alone, but if so the hope was short-lived. In early spring he was summoned again to Rome. Once more, the pope urged him to undertake the painting of the Sistine Chapel ceiling. Once more the artist resisted. But in the end he had no alternative but to swallow his disappointment about the tomb and do the pope's bidding. 'He went on refusing to such an extent, that the pope almost lost his temper,' writes Condivi. 'But when he saw that the pope was determined, he embarked on that work which is to be seen today in the papal palace to the admiration and amazement of the world, and which brought him so great a reputation that it set him above all envy.'

★   ★   ★

The chapel in which Michelangelo worked for the best part of four years is a simple rectangular building with heavily fortified

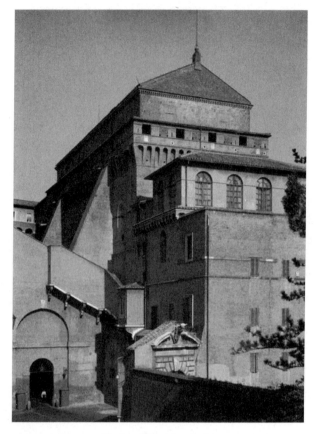

Sistine Chapel exterior

walls. It was designed by a Florentine architect named Baccio Pontelli during the pontificate of Julius II's uncle, Sixtus IV. Work began in 1477 and the building was finished by 1481, which suggests that its completion was viewed as a matter of considerable urgency by the papacy. The Sistine Chapel immediately became the principal place of worship for the *capella papalis*, or Papal Chapel, a corporate body consisting of the pope and about two hundred senior officials, drawn not only from the ranks of the Church hierarchy but also from the laity – it included cardinals,

the generals of the monastic and mendicant orders, visiting arch-
bishops and bishops, as well as qualifying members of the papal
household such as the sacristan, the major domo, chamberlains,
secretaries, notaries and auditors.[44]

As well as serving as a place of worship, the chapel also housed
the cardinals during the conclave in which every new pope was
elected. A conclave lasted several days and nights, during which
the cardinals would camp in the Sistine Chapel in temporary cells
erected for the purpose. Two rows of wooden-framed cubicles
were divided by a narrow passage. Each cubicle or cell was covered
in coloured cloth, purple for those cardinals created by the recently
deceased pope, green for the rest. According to a contemporary
eyewitness, when all the preparations for a conclave had been
made the Sistine Chapel resembled a hospital ward – a '*dormitorio
di hospitale*' – albeit one of a very splendid kind.[45]

The shape and size of the building mirrored its importance. Its
dimensions are those of Solomon's Temple, as they are described
in the Book of Kings. Its length is twice its height and three times
its width. The surfaces of Solomon's Temple were covered in
cedar and gold, but the Sistine Chapel was intended from the
outset to be decorated with paintings. As soon as the building was
ready Sixtus IV had commissioned leading artists of the time,
including Perugino, Signorelli and Botticelli, to paint two con-
tinuous fresco cycles on its walls. On one of the chapel's long
walls, they painted scenes from the life of Christ; on the other,
scenes from the life of Moses. The meaning of this parallelism is
underscored by inscriptions on the cornice declaring that Moses,
to whom God gave the Ten Commandments, 'is the bearer of the
Old Law', while Christ is 'the bearer of the new Law'.[46]

The pictures illustrated a commonplace of Christian theology,
one that underpinned the authority of the Church itself. They

insisted that the era of Mosaic law, or *tempus legis*, had been inevitably succeeded in God's plan by the era of Christ's unwritten law, which was the era of grace, or *tempus gratiae*. Directly above these frescoes, flanking the windows of the chapel, are depictions of the early popes. Arranged in chronological order, with each pope made to resemble a painted statue standing in a niche, they stress the continuity and legitimacy of the papal succession.

When Michelangelo was summoned by Julius II, the figurative paintings of the chapel stopped there. The shallow barrel vault of the ceiling was decorated with a rudimentary vision of heaven, an ultramarine sky with stars of gold that had been contributed by a minor artist called Piermatteo d'Amelia. But that was all.

The first scheme suggested to Michelangelo by the pope was surprisingly modest. It consisted principally of twelve depictions of the Apostles, to be painted on the twelve pendentives that run down between the six round-headed windows on each side of the chapel. Julius II, an enthusiastic connoisseur of the art of antiquity, also wanted Michelangelo to replace Piermatteo's starry sky with a modern version of the decorated ceilings that had been discovered in the recently excavated Golden House of the emperor Nero. The relatively undemanding nature of the proposal may only have strengthened Michelangelo's reluctance to carry it out. Twelve figures and a ceiling decorated with fashionably antique motifs, *grotteschi* and the like – this was hardly a fitting recompense for the loss of the commission for the great tomb.

By his own account, Michelangelo eventually plucked up his courage and told the pope exactly what he thought of his plan. It was, he said, 'a poor thing'. Unless he were allowed to do something much more ambitious, he would be wasting his own time and the pope's money. According to Michelangelo, Julius II capitulated, saying that the artist could do as he liked. Whether or not it happened exactly like that, it seems that Michelangelo was given considerable licence to reconceive the programme of paintings for the ceiling. Just as he had transformed a misshapen block of Carrara marble into the monumental *David*, so would he transform the pope's inchoate proposal into one of the most ambitious works of painting ever seen.

The new programme was far more complicated and far more extensive than the initial proposal. Michelangelo instantly did away with the idea of an essentially abstract decoration of the vault. Instead, it was to be decorated with nine depictions of stories from the Book of Genesis. The twelve Apostles in the pendentives were to be replaced by figures of the prophets and the sibyls who had told of the coming of Christ. Michelangelo also wanted to paint the arches above the windows with scenes showing Christ's ancestors. The artists employed by Sixtus IV had painted the lives of Christ and Moses, the eras of grace and of law. The theme of Michelangelo's new programme was the very first era of history, from God's creation of the world to the time of Noah. This was the era before that of Moses, known as *ante legem*, before the law. All in all, his scheme would both transform the chapel and complete it – turning the space into a total narrative of all human history as it was understood in Christian terms.

Michelangelo may have exaggerated when he said that the pope had given him licence to do as he liked. But like many of his other exaggerations and distortions, it may express something he felt to be morally if not literally true. The ceiling was *his*. He thought of it. He created it. It is very unlikely that he was actually given *carte blanche* in deciding the subject matter to be represented in the major chapel of the Vatican. The chances are that his proposals were at the very least vetted by Julius II and by one or more of the theologians in his circle. Yet the whole scheme bears the stamp of Michelangelo's powerfully idiosyncratic artistic personality. This is not just a matter of its scale, with 175 separate pictorial units replacing the mere twelve originally proposed. Its form, too, could only have been conceived by Michelangelo. He unified the many different parts of his scheme by arranging all of its images within the framework of a vast imaginary architectural structure. It resembles a classical temple, but most of all it resembles Michelangelo's earlier design for the project he had cherished above all others – that of the abandoned tomb for Julius II.[47]

Having persuaded the pope to agree to the new scheme, Michelangelo finally committed himself to the project. He hired a group of assistants from Florence, although he later told Condivi and Vasari that he soon became so dissatisfied with their standards of timekeeping and work that he locked them out of the chapel altogether, painting alone and 'without even the assistance of someone to grind his colours for him'. This cannot be strictly true, because even an artist as independent as Michelangelo cannot have dispensed with the services of a colour-grinder and a plasterer, whose job it would have been to prepare the *intonaco*, the layer of wet plaster on which each day's painting was to be done. This is another of Michelangelo's eloquent half-truths – his way of letting posterity know that he delegated little of the actual painting of the vault to anyone else, which was certainly the case.

Michelangelo was also responsible for the ingenious design of the scaffolding necessary for the work. He devised a structure which in Vasari's description was 'erected on supports which kept clear of the walls' – a wooden platform resting on joists wedged into a series of holes cut into the walls above the chapel windows, which allowed the building to remain in use during the years that Michelangelo spent painting the vault. The platform was half the vault's length, so halfway through the work it was moved from one end of the chapel to the other. According to Vasari, Michelangelo's economical design replaced an earlier, unsuccessful structure, supported by ropes, that had been cobbled together by the pope's architect Bramante. In this way, Vasari says, he 'enabled a poor carpenter, who rebuilt the scaffolding, to dispense with so many of the ropes that when Michelangelo gave him what was left over he sold them and made enough money for a dowry for his daughter'.

Contrary to legend, Michelangelo did not paint the vault of the chapel lying down. There was room between platform and ceiling for the artist to stand, and that was how he worked, although such was the angle at which he had to crane his neck that he suffered constantly from cramps, spasms and headaches. He wrote a comical poem about the experience, which he dedicated to a friend, a man called Giovanni (John) who lived in Pistoia, but about whom nothing else is known; and he embellished it with a tiny caricature of a painter – himself – reaching upwards to the ceiling with his brush (see p. ii).

> I've got myself a goitre from this strain,
> As water gives the cats in Lombardy
> Or maybe it is in some other country;
> My belly's pushed by force beneath my chin.
>
> My beard toward Heaven, I feel the back of my brain
> Upon my neck, I grow the breast of a Harpy;
> My brush, above my face continually,
> Makes it a splendid floor by dripping down.
>
> My loins have penetrated to my paunch,
> My rump's a crupper, as a counterweight,
> And pointless the unseeing steps I go.

In front of me my skin is being stretched
While it folds up behind and forms a knot,
And I am bending like a Syrian bow.

And judgement, hence, must grow,
Borne in the mind, peculiar and untrue;
You cannot shoot well when the gun's askew.

John, come to the rescue
Of my dead painting now, and of my honour;
I'm not in a good place, and I'm no painter.[48]

★　　★　　★

The rest of this book is about the paintings created by the man who thought he was no painter.

PART TWO

The Sistine Chapel Ceiling

The nine narrative paintings that run the length of the ceiling, from above the altar to above the main entrance of the chapel, tell stories drawn from the Book of Genesis. Their subjects are all-encompassing: the origin of the universe; the origin of Man; the origin of evil and the nature of life, as it must be lived, in the world after the Fall. They are arranged by Michelangelo into three triads, or groups of three. The first triad shows God creating the universe and the world. The second shows the creation of Adam and Eve, their falling into temptation in the garden of Eden, and their expulsion from paradise. The third tells the story of Noah, recounting the dark story of the deluge and giving an equally dark account of the beginnings of human history. Between them, these works go to the heart of Michelangelo's intensely powerful, idiosyncratic spirituality and reveal the full extent of his genius as a painter.

The nine narrative paintings are like nine vertebrae forming a single spine. But Michelangelo's fresco cycle does not only tell stories from Genesis. It also shows images of the prophets, the sibyls and the Saviour's ancestors. Taken in its entirety, it amounts to a synthesis of all biblical history before the advent of Christ.

It is an obvious fact, but one worth re-emphasising, that

Michelangelo's paintings frame this great span of pre-Christian history from a Christian perspective. The assertion of Christ's central salvific role in God's plan for erring humanity is explicit in the very nature of the Sistine Chapel as a grand arena for ceremonial papal masses – a place where the pope himself, and his cardinals, mystically partake of the flesh and blood of the Saviour. Christ is directly represented only once in the paintings of the ceiling, as an infant pre-existing in the mind of God, among the group clustered together within God's mantle in *The Creation of Adam*. But Christ's life and death are prefigured throughout Michelangelo's nine Genesis narratives. Several of the scenes have been carefully designed to allude to Christ's sacrifice on the Cross, the wounding of his flesh and the spilling of his blood. It is a general truth about Michelangelo's painting that the forms and figures within it are constantly shadowed by their own potential for metamorphosis, so that stories that seem to be about one thing may also be about another.

Such prefigurings of Christ take many forms on the ceiling, some of which would have been obvious to Michelangelo's contemporaries. It was a commonplace of medieval and Renaissance theology, for example, to refer to Christ as 'a second Adam' – expressing the symmetry by which God's incarnation as a mortal man, in the person of Jesus Christ, held out the possibility of mankind's ultimate salvation from the consequences of Adam's original sin. So it is that the sleeping figure of Adam, in Michelangelo's depiction of *The Creation of Eve*, anticipates the crumpled figure of the dead Christ awaiting entombment; and so it is that the cruciform shape made by the Tree of Knowledge and the arm of the avenging angel, in *The Temptation and Expulsion*, prefigures that of the Cross on which Christ would be crucified.

By finding such foreshadowings of the New Testament in the

stories of the Old Testament, Michelangelo and those who may have helped him in the design of his fresco cycle were doing something that Christians had done since the dawn of their faith. In the first century of the Christian era, as a result of Paul's mission to the Gentiles, Paul and the early Church fathers had reinterpreted the entire Jewish tradition in the light of their own beliefs. It was their contention that all of the scattered stories of the Hebraic biblical tradition might be drawn together within a single concept of universal history. The heroes of the Old Testament were recast as a succession of figures whose actions and legends prognosticated the appearance of Christ. The words of the texts telling their stories were interrogated by generation on generation of patristic commentators for any sign that might be read as a concealed, secret portent of the coming of Christ.

The credo that underpinned this ancient tradition of interpretation is summed up by the words of an inscription placed by a master theologian of the French Middle Ages, Abbot Denis Suger, on the Concordance Window of the abbey of Saint Denis: '*Quod Moses velat Christi doctrina revelat*', 'What Moses veils, the doctrine of Christ reveals'. In other words, the Old Testament contains the truth as revealed to Moses and the prophets, but partially hidden, as by a veil. Only through the revelation of Christ's words and deeds can the full truth of God's plan for mankind begin to be grasped.

Even before Michelangelo ever worked there, this same structure of belief was written into the Sistine Chapel, just as it had been into the window of Suger's Norman abbey. The series of frescoes at ground level, painted in the late fifteenth century by a number of masters including Botticelli and Perugino, compare and contrast the life of Moses with that of Christ. The message is the same: *Quod Moses velat Christi doctrina revelat.*[1]

The notion of a mystical concordance between the Old and the New Testaments, so strongly emphasised by the earlier paintings in the Sistine Chapel, is also integral to Michelangelo's fresco cycle. This is made clear by the presence of the prophets and the sibyls, those individuals from Judaic and pagan history who were held to have foretold the birth of Christ. These figures all appear in the lower register of his design for the ceiling, with the nine Old Testament narratives seeming to float above them. Both literally and figuratively, the painter's telling of the Genesis stories is sustained by belief in a vision of universal history that has, at its centre and as its climax, the redemptive sacrifice of Christ.

It is important to understand and to respect the Christian beliefs and traditions which Michelangelo strove to express for three long years of his life. But it is equally important to remember that the Sistine Chapel ceiling is a great work of art precisely because it does much more than give visible form to a particular set of religious orthodoxies. The pictures of the ceiling stunned and impressed the artist's contemporaries not only because they were so accomplished but also because they were so deeply unorthodox and original.

In almost every one of the Sistine ceiling's many compositions, Michelangelo departed from tried and trusted pictorial convention. He told the stories in his own way and embodied them in his own particular language, a form of painting in which representation has been pared down to almost nothing but the figure, nude or clothed (but most frequently nude). He used the human form, in action and reaction, to express a vast range of feelings and ideas and spiritual aspirations. Many of those feelings and ideas can be explained, to a certain extent, by reference to Christian theology. But throughout the ceiling's rich weave of imagery there are subtleties of allusion, visual echoes and rhymes, suggestions and half-suggestions that go beyond the straight-forward expression of Christian doctrine.

I

The Genesis Cycle, first triad: *The Separation of Light and Darkness*; *The Creation of the Sun, Moon and Plants*; *The Creation of Life in the Waters*

Michelangelo begins at the beginning, with a depiction of *The Separation of Light and Darkness*. He shows the Almighty God of the Old Testament as a heroic male figure with grey beard and hair, dressed in lilac robes that swirl about him, twisting upwards through the heavens to separate light from darkness. He embodies male strength but also the fecundity of the female principle, in that Michelangelo has given him pectoral muscles nearly as rounded as a woman's breasts. The figure rises into space amid rays of light. The picture is at once the sparest and the most austere of the ceiling's scenes of Creation.

The subject is drawn from the Book of Genesis:

> In the beginning God created the heaven and the earth. And the earth was without form, and void; and darkness was upon the face of the deep. And the Spirit of God moved upon the face of the waters. And God said, Let there be light: and there was light. And God saw the light, that it was good: and God divided the light from the darkness. And God called the light Day, and the darkness he called Night. And the evening and the morning were the first day. (Genesis 1: 1-5)

There was no precedent in earlier Christian art for Michelangelo's dynamic airborne deity swooping through an implied

infinity of space. The artists of the Byzantine and medieval traditions had expressed their own sense of the ineffable mystery of
God the Creator by removing the scenes so elliptically described
at the start of Genesis to a pictorial world of abstract geometrical
perfection. The Italo-Byzantine craftsmen who had created the
thirteenth-century mosaics of the dome of the Baptistry in
Florence – a famous and much venerated building at the heart
of the town where Michelangelo spent his formative years –
had represented the God of the Creation scenes as a solemn,
hieratic figure floating on a ground of gold, enclosed by the
celestial spheres, making a stiff gesture of benediction. The
artists of the early Renaissance had humanised God the Father,
to the extent that he could appear in Masaccio's celebrated
fresco of *The Trinity*, of the 1420s, in the Florentine church of
Santa Maria Novella, as a doughty ancient with a forbiddingly
solemn expression on his face. But Michelangelo energised this
still recently anthropomorphised figure in a way that was both
new and revolutionary.

His reinvention of the all-creating deity as a figure flying
through space under the unseen impulse of divine will, was to
prove enormously influential. Artists of the High Renaissance
such as Raphael, followed by the painters of the Baroque and
Rococo periods, would follow Michelangelo in embodying God
as a being with human form endowed with a superhuman,
cosmic thrust and energy. Romantic painters of the eighteenth
and nineteenth centuries would impart something of his twisting,
irrepressible force to the Promethean heroes of their own disenchanted mythologies. Michelangelo's influence can even be
discerned in the popular art of the twentieth century. Inventors
of the American superhero comic-strip adapted his style to their
own ends. The character of Superman has his origins, as a graphic

creation, in the airborne God who flies majestically across the Sistine Chapel ceiling.

Although *The Separation of Light and Darkness* is the first of the nine narrative scenes from the Book of Genesis, Michelangelo painted it last of all, along with the other two scenes of primal creation. Having gradually worked his way along the ceiling, starting at the chapel's entrance with the painted histories of fallen humanity, he finished above the altar with images of the all-powerful God. So while the momentum of his narrative moves, as in the Old Testament, from the acts of God to the life of man, Michelangelo actually *painted* that narrative in reverse order. There could have been purely practical reasons for this, but the artist's piety may also have played a part. Michelangelo must have known that, as he proceeded with the project, he would become more technically accomplished in the medium of fresco. Perhaps he wanted to be at his best when painting the scenes that involved God alone.

To create the image of the deity reaching up to separate light from darkness, night from day, Michelangelo used the difficult technique known as *sotto in sù*. The figure is seen, from beneath, as though soaring up and away from the viewer. Practical methods had been devised by earlier generations of artists for accomplishing this particular type of illusion. The architect and theorist Leon Battista Alberti, in his treatise on painting of the 1430s, had described a perspective 'veil' – a grid of threads strung on a wooden frame, through which a painter might study a subject seen at an extreme angle of foreshortening, transcribing each element of what he saw on to the corresponding sections of a squared-up piece of paper. If Michelangelo used a device of that kind, he did not do so slavishly. Such was his self-assurance that he departed in many details from the carefully calculated sketch for this scene produced in his workshop, to help him realise this difficult perspectival illusion. The outlines of that sketch were incised into the wet plaster before Michelangelo began work, so the evidence still survives of just how freely he improvised from it. Minute study of the picture's surface during conservation has revealed that the artist changed the angle and position of both of God's hands and arms, and even shifted the entire figure so as to set it more firmly on a diagonal – increasing its torsion and intensifying the sense of God's upwardly spiralling energy.

The difficulty of making off-the-cuff changes to such a challenging composition should not be underestimated. It is a tribute to Michelangelo's exceptional ability to think three-dimensionally, even when working in two dimensions, that he managed to carry it off. It is as if, in painting *The Separation of Light and Darkness*, he conceived the rectangular panel to be painted not as a flat surface but as a block of stone extending upwards through the vault of the ceiling. Into that block, he imagined himself carving the figure of God, painting a form he could almost feel with his hands.

God's act of creation is simultaneously an act of division. He reaches into the air as though separating bright swirls of lightly tinted steam from a mass of heavy grey stormclouds. Michelangelo, as well as the more theologically learned among his audience, may have associated the separation of light from darkness with ideas about the Creation expressed by the venerable Saint Augustine (354–430). In *The City of God*, the influence of which had been all-pervasive in medieval Christendom, Augustine had compared God's separation of day from night to his division of the angels into two communities, the good and the bad. A number of traditions told of the rebel angels rising against God, under the leadership of Lucifer, and being cast down into darkness by the host of good angels, led by the Archangel Michael. Augustine explicitly identified the good angels with heaven and the light that God called 'Day' in Genesis 1: 1 and 1: 3–5. The all-creating God is also God the judge. Just as, in the beginning, he divided dark from light, good from evil, so on the last day will he divide mankind into the saved and the damned.

★   ★   ★

There are numerous stories of Julius's growing impatience with the length of time it took to finish the ceiling. On one occasion, he is even said to have struck Michelangelo in a fit of frustrated rage.[2] The pope's importunity may explain the great speed with which the artist finished the scenes of the Creation. Not only were they among the last to be completed, they were by some distance the most rapidly painted. Analysis of its surface has revealed that *The Separation of Light and Darkness* was painted in a single *giornata* – just one working day of about eight hours, a period determined by the rapid drying-time of the wet plaster into which the painter of true fresco is obliged to work his images. The artist worked quickly and instinctively, using particularly dilute pigment so that in places the figure of God seems as though dissolving into – or condensing out of – the circumambient air.

As a measure of the painter's acceleration, the time taken three years earlier to paint *The Deluge*, at the other end of the chapel, had been no fewer than twenty-nine separate *giornate*. Admittedly, the subjects are hardly comparable, in that *The Deluge* occupies a larger area of ceiling and contains many different figures, all of whom had to be depicted in some detail for the story to make its impact. The broad, summary style in which Michelangelo painted the soaring figure of God was well adapted to the contrasting grandeur of the opening of Genesis – a metaphor, itself, for the sweeping, flowing, creative powers of divinity.

★   ★   ★

Michelangelo also worked with great rapidity on the second of
the three scenes of primal Creation. This was a larger and more
complicated composition than *The Separation of Light and Darkness*,
but one that still took him only seven *giornate* to complete. Its
subject is *The Creation of the Sun, Moon and Plants*. This time the
figure of God appears twice, to indicate that two different
moments in the narrative have been telescoped together.

To the right, frowning with concentration, he divides the
heavens with a sweeping gesture of his arms, creating both sun
and moon. The wingless angels in his broad cape express a mixture
of admiration and awe, bordering on terror. This part of the
composition is drawn from Genesis 1: 14–18: 'And God said let
there be lights in the firmament of the heaven to divide the day
from the night ... And God made two great lights; the greater
light to rule the day, and the lesser light to rule the night. . .'

To the left he is seen from behind. Here, the contours and
delicate colouring of God's lilac robe give it the look of a conch
shell flying unexpectedly through the sky. He is shown in the act
of bringing forth vegetation from the hitherto barren earth, in
the form of a few wisps of grass and fronds of fern, silhouetted
against the white air. Michelangelo's source here was Genesis 1:
11: 'And God said let the earth bring forth grass, the herb yielding
seed, and the fruit tree yielding fruit, whose seed was in itself . . .'

There is a pointed lack of emphasis on the actual creation of
the earth, a part of the story that the artist has not quite left out
but has certainly abbreviated to a bare minimum. It is implied, so
to speak, as something that *must necessarily have happened*, in the
gesture with which the receding figure of God calls forth the
grasses and other plants. But even that gesture is given relatively
little prominence, enacted as it is by a Creator whose mighty

back – and even mightier posterior – is turned to the spectator. Far greater prominence is given to the formation of the sun and moon. Both were drawn with the aid of a compass – the imprint made by its point is still minutely visible in the centre of each sphere – and coloured in flat thin layers of golden yellow and silvery grey. Michelangelo has contrived matters so that his entire composition revolves around sun and moon and the divine gesture that links them.

According to an ancient tradition going back at least as far as to the writings of the fourth-century St Ambrose, the sun was held to be a mystic symbol of Christ, while the moon, reflecting back the sun's radiance, was equated with the Virgin Mary, mother of Christ and embodiment of the Church. In creating the sun and moon, therefore, God was also pre-ordaining Christ's Incarnation and the institution of the Church. His outflung arms are a visual anticipation of Christ's arms, stretched upon the Cross. The expression of solemnity on his face suggests that even at this moment, so close to the beginning of time, he is gazing ahead and seeing, in his mind's eye, the betrayal and death of his son.

★   ★   ★

In the last painting of the first triad, Michelangelo's God is restored once more to effortless tranquillity. He floats through the air, again wrapped in a billowing mantle and attended by a small angelic retinue. This time he is shown above a vast expanse of greyish-white water. Some authors have assumed that the painter had Genesis 1: 2 in mind: 'And the Spirit of God moved upon the face of the waters.' Others believe that he meant to indicate the separation of the land from the water, as it is described in Genesis 1: 6: 'And God said let there be a firmament in the midst of the waters, and let it divide the waters from the waters.'

Either hypothesis, if true, would mean that Michelangelo had disturbed the chronology of Genesis in the order of his pictures. But there is no good reason to suppose that the artist reversed biblical time here. The last of his three pictures almost certainly depicts the events of the fourth day of Creation, which take place directly *after* the creation of sun and moon: 'And the evening and the morning were the fourth day. And God said, Let the waters bring forth abundantly the moving creatures that have life ...' The gesture of his hands suggests that Michelangelo chose to paint the very moment of this invocation. God holds his palms above the water, creating a teeming multitude of unseen creatures down in the depths of the ocean.

II

The Genesis Cycle, second triad: *The Creation of Adam*; *The Creation of Eve*; *The Temptation and Expulsion from Paradise*

The ceiling's central triad of images begins with *The Creation of Adam*, a majestic depiction of the moment when God imparts life and a soul to the first of men. It is among the most dynamic and startlingly original of all Michelangelo's inventions. Like many famous pictures, it can all too easily be taken for granted. The overwhelming familiarity of the composition, its beguiling power and simplicity, can obscure its true qualities. Only on close, careful inspection does the work disclose its range of meanings and subtleties of expression.

The tradition of misreading *The Creation of Adam* is as old as the picture itself. So far did it depart from all previous artists' imaginings of the creation of humanity that the work completely bemused at least one early visitor to the Sistine Chapel. Paolo Giovio, bishop of Nocera, who also wrote brief lives of Raphael and Leonardo da Vinci, composed a slender biographical sketch of Michelangelo some time between 1523 and 1527. Giovio's text, a bare 31 lines in Latin, contains a short appreciation of the Sistine Chapel ceiling, which is principally memorable for revealing the author's bafflement when faced with *The Creation of Adam*: 'Among the most important figures is that of an old man, in the middle of the ceiling, who is represented in the act of flying through the air . . .'[3] Giovio clearly had no idea of what he was looking at. But his incomprehension serves as a measure of just how novel, how alien to prevailing conventions, Michelangelo's painting seemed to his contemporaries.

The artist was familiar with other depictions of the same theme by earlier Renaissance artists. In devising his composition, he may have had somewhere in his mind a celebrated bronze panel by Jacopo della Quercia on the Porta Magna of San Petronio, in Bologna, a city Michelangelo knew well, having spent several months there creating his doomed monumental bronze portrait of Pope Julius II. Jacopo had depicted Adam nude and recumbent on a somewhat abstract outcrop of rock, springing into life as if waking from sleep, with the cloaked figure of God the Father standing over him, making a restrained, priestly gesture of benediction. Michelangelo galvanised this somewhat wooden piece of early Renaissance theatre by turning it into a whirlwind encounter between man and God. The Almighty floats weightlessly through space, wrapped in a billowing red cloak that enfolds his angelic entourage. He is a severe, grey-bearded Creator, reaching out with great deliberation towards the languid Adam, a suitably earthbound figure (the name 'Adam' is also the Hebrew word for 'earth'). So it is that God imparts to man, across the few inches of air that separate their outstretched fingers, the spark of life that makes him move and breathe.

In early Christian depictions of the creation of man, God had usually been truncated to a mere hand gesturing from a strategically placed cloud. He had developed into the familiar figure of an old man with a beard by the middle of the fifteenth century, but there was no precedent for showing him 'in the act of flying through the air', let alone dressed in clinging draperies that reveal his legs from the thigh down. The fingertip act of creation was also Michelangelo's own invention. Given that this has become the single most famous, most reproduced detail in the entire pictorial scheme of the ceiling – despite the fact that the celebrated fingertips themselves were repainted, due to a small area of loss, by the restorer Domenico Carnevale in the 1570s – it is worth considering in some depth just what Michelangelo may have intended by it.

Where did the painter get this striking idea? It owes little to the account given in Genesis 2: 7, which casts God in the role of a sculptor who literally breathes life into his work: 'The Lord God formed man, of dust from the ground, and breathed into his nostrils the breath of life.' Michelangelo may have taken inspiration from a medieval hymn traditionally sung at Vespers on Whit Sunday, one stanza of which refers to '*Digitus paternae dexterae*' – the finger of God's right hand. The overarching theme of this hymn, which celebrates the nature of God's gifts to man, also seems apposite to *The Creation of Adam*:

> The seven-fold gift of grace is thine,
> Thou finger of the hand divine;
> The Father's promise true, to teach
> Our earthly tongues thy heavenly speech.
>
> Thy light to every sense impart;
> Pour forth thy love in every heart;

Our weakened flesh do thou restore
To strength and courage evermore.

Drive far away our spirits' foe,
Thine own abiding peace bestow;
If thou dost go before as guide,
No evil can our steps betide.

The notion that God, through the touch of his finger, meta-phorically imparts not only grace but also instruction was embed-ded in earlier Christian tradition. In considering the Ten Commandments given to Moses from on high, Church fathers had seized on the metaphor of a divine finger – one that both writes instructions for mankind and points out the path of the true and good life. St Augustine develops this idea in a passage in his fifth-century treatise *De spiritu et littera*:

> That Holy Spirit, through whom charity which is the fulness of the law is shed abroad in our hearts, is also called in the Gospel the finger of God. That those tables of the law were written by the finger of God, and that the finger of God is God's spirit through whom we are sanctified, so that living by faith we may do good works through love . . .[4]

It is impossible to prove that Michelangelo, or the papal advisers who may have helped him to formulate his iconography, had such ideas in mind when devising *The Creation of Adam*. Interpretations of paintings based on their presumed connections to a specific text or texts are often suspect. This is especially true when those texts are not the primary sources, as in this case, but are drawn instead from the deep well of post-biblical Christian thought. Such hypotheses bring with them the temptation to force ill-fitting meanings on to works of art that visually resist them – to yoke the unwilling image to the inflexible word. As Leo Steinberg once cuttingly remarked of a fellow art historian, 'His glimpse of a Michelangelo picture is as from a speeding car bound for the library.' Yet in this particular instance the facts of the picture seem to confirm rather than contradict the hypothesis – suggesting that Michelangelo was indeed aware of the Christian tradition that found, in the image of God's finger, a metaphor for his commands.

There is a look of total concentration on the face of the creating God, in Michelangelo's fresco. But his gaze, depicted with such sharpness and clarity, is pointedly *not* directed at the reclining Adam. Instead, he stares with great intensity at his own outstretched finger. He does so in a way that suggests that what is being channelled through it, and towards Adam, is not only the impulse of life but also man's incipient awareness of God's own will – and, with that, the capacity for thought and for moral action. It is as if, in the moment of his creation, Adam is also being instructed in the laws by which God means him to live – laws that he will break, with fatal consequences for all of mankind.

Did Michelangelo really mean the viewer to understand all this, in the gesture and gaze of the Almighty? There are good reasons for believing so. The idea of transgression, Adam's transgression against the divine will, is central to the tragic unfolding of the Genesis story as told by the artist. In the next painting but one, *The Temptation and Expulsion*, he will take the forbidden fruit. Michelangelo will later make it clear that man's fallen condition is a direct consequence of Adam's disobedience, by making the slumped body of the drunken Noah – the epitome of postlapsarian human frailty – resemble a pathetically collapsed version of Adam's God-perfected body in the scene of his creation. Yet for Adam to transgress, Adam must first be given the laws that he is to break. This begs the question, where, if not in *The Creation of Adam*, does Michelangelo imply that narratively necessary divine act of instruction? There is no space for it anywhere else in his scheme. The subject of the painting is best understood, therefore, as the formation rather than simply the creation of man.

The most compelling evidence for this interpretation is to be found in one of the most obvious places, namely Ascanio Condivi's life of the artist. Admittedly, Condivi is an occasionally unreliable witness, but the fact remains that he knew Michelangelo intimately, and the very terseness of his description of *The Creation of Adam*, so pointedly bald and unembroidered as it is, gives it all the more credibility. Of the figure of the Almighty, Condivi simply writes the following: 'God is seen with arm and hand outstretched as if to impart to Adam the precepts as to what he must and must not do.'[5]

Michelangelo's Adam looks up at God with an expression of barely dawning awareness on his face. He has just woken into consciousness and there is still about him the wide-eyed helplessness of a child. Yet the look in his eyes suggests that he has already begun to absorb the awareness that life brings with it duty to God. There is a slight implication of melancholy in his gaze, as of someone being drawn half against their will from blissful ignorance towards a sense of responsibility.

Adam's body is full-grown and athletic. The chiselled outlines, the ebbs and flows of contour that define his nude form, recall Walter Pater's famous remark about art aspiring to the condition of music. The effect of the entire figure is epitomised by the single detail of Adam's outstretched arm – which swells and fades, rises and falls, from the curve of the shoulder to the soft bump of the bicep, along the meandering line of the forearm and across the reaching hand, like a melody drawn in the air.

The modelling of the figure's flesh and muscles in light and

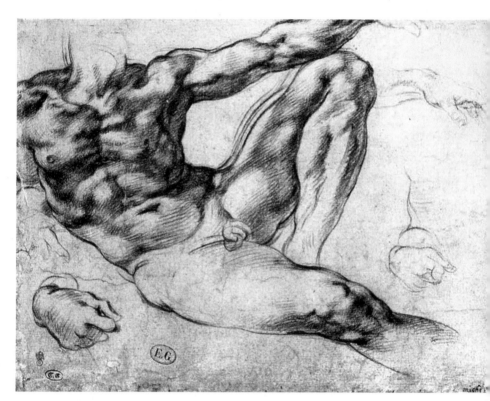

Study for The Creation of Adam

shade is equally haunting (and represents a triumph of subtlety within the medium of fresco, which is far less malleable and forgiving than oil paint, making such effects of chiaroscuro notably difficult to achieve). Michelangelo disdained landscape painting but here he has painted Adam's body as if the human form were itself a landscape to be explored. The soft juncture of his left calf and thigh, the shadowy hollows and protuberances formed in the area around his neck and collarbone, are painted with an immense, tender sensuality. They have what the twentieth-century painter Frank Auerbach has called a 'haptic' quality, a term denoting painted forms so instinct with life that to look at them is to have the uncanny sense of physically touching that which is depicted.

Adam must be perfect, his image that of a god on earth, because of the words of Genesis 1: 26: 'And God said, Let us make man in our image, after our likeness.' In no other figure on the whole of the ceiling is Adam's beauty repeated, and that too is part of Michelangelo's expressive purpose. The first of men, newly created, represents a perfect state of harmony with God – but one that is destined to be lost, and never recaptured until the blessed rise on the day of the resurrection.

The scene where the action takes place is the most abstracted of landscapes, a grassy mound suspended in infinite space. Temporally, the picture is even more ambiguous because it represents a moment in which all of history – from the creation of man to his fall and ultimate salvation – is also contained. Michelangelo gives to God an aspect that expresses his infinite power. The vivid coils and whorls of his hair and beard evoke the cataclysmic patterns of whirlwinds and whirlpools. They bear a remarkably close resemblance to a later, celebrated group of apocalyptic drawings of floods and deluges by Michelangelo's contemporary (and occasional rival) Leonardo da Vinci, who knew the Sistine Chapel and may have been influenced by this detail.

The figures contained within God's mantle span the arc of time. At his shoulder he is accompanied by seraphim and cherubim, members of the highest order of the angels, to whom Michelangelo has also given the character of classical representations of the four winds. Their presence makes of the mantle a sail, swelled by their breath and thus impelled through space. Below God's right arm lies a mysterious, anguished figure, present only as a groaning face, half obscured by darkness. This shadowy presence can tentatively be identified as a personification of Chaos, the dark nothingness from which the Almighty wrestled the universe into being – now conquered, he is whirled along in God's train like the captives trailed in the wake of ancient triumphal processions.

There is also a beautiful young woman held in the embrace of God's left arm. She looks across at Adam with a lively, fascinated gaze – the look, almost, of a startled gazelle – suggesting that she knows her destiny to be entwined with his. She can be identified with certainty. She is Eve, preordained in the mind of God from the beginning. Michelangelo has arranged his composition so that she appears as if coming out of God's left side, a subtle pre-figuration of the way in which she will actually emerge from the left side of Adam – God's own likeness on earth – in the ceiling's very next narrative scene. The length of green drapery that enfolds her loins has become unwound and flutters freely in the air beneath the crowded mantle of divinity, reaching down towards the earth that is Adam's namesake. Green is the colour of life, symbolising Eve's fruitfulness as the future mother of mankind.

If the spectator looking up at the ceiling should choose at this point to zoom out, so to speak, and encompass all three of Michelangelo's paintings telling the story of Adam and Eve, a larger pattern of meaning can be seen to have its origin here. The figure of Eve is repeated twice more across a single, powerful diagonal that connects all three narrative scenes of the ceiling's central triad – creating, as it were, one line of vision along which can be traced the successive stages of her destiny. She nestles in God's mantle; she emerges from Adam's side; she tempts Adam to his fall.

Behind the figure of Eve, in *The Creation of Adam*, can be glimpsed another female figure, with wispy blonde hair and a face partially obscured by paint damage. Her hand is wrapped around God's left arm, suggesting her proximity to the Almighty. The most likely explanation for this figure's presence is to be found in Proverbs, Chapter 8, in which Wisdom is personified as a woman coeval with God himself. 'The Lord possessed me in the beginning of his way, before his works of old,' she proclaims. 'I was set up from everlasting, from the beginning, or ever the earth there was ... When he prepared the heavens I was there, when he set a compass upon the face of the depth' (Proverbs 8: 22–7). Wisdom seems to be leaning forward to whisper into Eve's ear. But Eve, transfixed by the sight of her husband, pays her no heed.

Numerous interlinked allusions and associations play across the composition. These form a chain of meaning, carried from figure to figure, at times from hand to hand, the end of which is to create a metaphor for an omniscient God's all-encompassing salvific plan for erring humanity. In the figure of Eve is also implied that of the Virgin Mary, vessel of the Incarnation. Beside her is a staring child, a look of ominous foreboding in his eyes. He is the infant Jesus Christ – an identification underlined by the hand of God, whose fingers encircle the round protuberance of the child's right shoulder in just the same gesture used by a priest when he elevates the Host, flesh of Christ, at the ceremony of the Mass. Within the mantle of God, within the divine mind, all is foretold and all foreseen.

★ ★ ★

The second of Michelangelo's paintings telling the story of Adam and Eve is *The Creation of Eve*, the biblical source for which is Genesis 2: 21–2: 'And the Lord God caused a deep sleep to fall upon Adam, and he slept; and he took one of his ribs, and closed up the flesh instead thereof; And the rib, which the Lord God had taken from man, made he a woman ...' The artist shows the blonde-haired Eve emerging from the side of Adam and coming face to face with her creator. Michelangelo has placed Adam's sleeping form next to a jumble of dark rocks, which introduces a spatial ambiguity into the scene and makes Eve look as though she might be stepping from the entrance of a cave beside him. Emerging from darkness into light, she seems astonished by the suddenness of her encounter with God. Her mouth hangs half open in amazement and she holds her hands up instinctively in a prayer that also looks like a gesture of supplication. With his raised right hand, God seems to be pulling her upright, drawing her out of Adam's side and into life. He stares solemnly into her troubled eyes.

The figure of God in *The Creation of Eve* is distinctly less awe-inspiring than the airborne, cosmic creator of the earlier Genesis scenes. Dressed in a voluminous mantle, he has here the aspect of a patriarch or priest. He does not fly, but stands and even stoops slightly in the act of creating woman. His weight upon the earth is suggested by the single mighty foot shown protruding from his robes, toes splayed on the bare grey ground. His hair and beard are a lank, dullish blond, painted with far less energy and animation than the swirling grey locks of God in the other scenes.

How can these differences be explained? Partly, perhaps, as a result of the evolution of Michelangelo's ideas between one phase of painting and the next. The artist was to break off from painting the ceiling for several months after finishing *The Creation of Eve*. This pause for thought might well account for the great difference between the figure of God the Father as he appears in this picture, and as he would appear in the three scenes of the creation of the universe and *The Creation of Adam*.

It may simply be that Michelangelo, recognising that God would have to become dynamically more active for the earlier scenes of creation, took the chance offered by a break in his work to reconceive his personification of the deity. But one of the great (and relatively underrated) aspects of the artist's achievement in painting the Sistine Chapel ceiling was that he managed to preserve the total unity of the scheme despite the evolution of his own style during the course of the four years that it took him to complete it. And the fact remains that the character of God, as he appears in *The Creation of Eve*, powerfully contributes to the particular expressive twist that Michelangelo gives to this episode in the Genesis story.

The position of the fresco on the ceiling of the chapel is significant. It is the central image of the nine narrative scenes, occupying a place directly above the screen that once divided the area closest to the altar – reserved for the pope and his court – from that occupied by less exalted worshippers. It marks a corresponding separation within the overall scheme of the Genesis narrative, dividing the stories of creation from those of fallen humanity. So it makes sense that the figure of God should suddenly, in this image, seem so much more grounded. This is the moment when the story itself comes decisively to earth. The transition is not a joyful one. The action takes place on a lonely stretch of coast. The line of the horizon, where sea meets sky, neatly bisects Eve's body at the midriff.

The overt symbolism of the picture restates the ultimate beneficence of God's plan for mankind. The sleeping Adam, beneath a dead tree stump suggestive of a truncated cross, is once more a prefiguration of Christ, while Eve, springing from his side, calls to mind the sacraments of baptism and the Eucharist, in that water and blood ran from the side of the crucified Christ (associations reinforced by the water behind her, and by the way in which she holds her hands up to the priest-like figure of God, like a worshipper at Mass preparing to receive the wafer). But the pious complacency inherent in such typologies is disturbed by the raw emotion with which the painting is charged. A current of intense, troubled feeling courses from Eve to the Almighty. She looks at God with an expression of pained and pleading mystery that lends this already cramped and claustrophobic act of creation an ominous, menacing atmosphere.

Eve, placed dead centre of the entire Sistine Chapel ceiling, is given a unique privilege. She is the only figure on the whole ceiling who is allowed to look into the eyes of God. Does she already feel sinfulness stirring within her breast? Could she be asking God *why* he has made her, *why* he has squeezed her into being, imperfect as she is? These are among the oldest and most intractable questions that Christians have asked themselves about their God. If all was foreknown, all foreordained, by a perfectly benevolent deity, why create the possibility of evil at all? But in Michelangelo's painting, she receives no answer. The solemn God stares back at Eve with eyes as hard, as unyielding, as stones.

★   ★   ★

The last scene in the central triad of images on the ceiling is *The Temptation and Expulsion*. Here Michelangelo tells the story of the

Fall of Man, giving his own narrative interpretation to the events recounted in the Book of Genesis, Chapter 3.

First, Adam and Eve fall into temptation in the Garden of Eden, and are punished for their sin:

> Now the serpent was more subtil than any beast of the field which the Lord God had made. And he said unto the woman, Yea, hath God said, Ye shall not eat of every tree of the garden? And the woman said unto the serpent, We may eat of the fruit of the trees of the garden: But of the fruit of the tree which is in the midst of the garden, God hath said, Ye shall not eat of it, neither shall ye touch it, lest ye die. And the serpent said unto the woman, Ye shall not surely die: For God doth know that in the day ye eat thereof, then your eyes shall be opened, and ye shall be as gods, knowing good and evil. And when the woman saw that the tree was good for food, and that it was pleasant to the eyes, and a tree to be desired to make one wise, she took of the fruit thereof, and did eat, and gave also unto her husband with her; and he did eat. (Genesis 3: 1–6)

Then, God discovers Adam's transgression and condemns him and Eve to suffer the pains, labour and discord of mortal life. To ensure that Adam does not take fruit also from the tree of life, and become immortal, God exiles him for ever from Eden:

> Therefore the Lord God sent him forth from the garden of Eden, to till the ground from whence he was taken. So he drove out the man; and he placed at the east of the garden of Eden Cherubims, and a flaming sword which turned every way, to keep the way of the tree of life. (Genesis 3: 23–4)

Generations of artists before Michelangelo had depicted these two scenes separately. Going against convention, he joined them in a single image, framed with such fearful symmetry that it links the crime with its punishment in a pattern of stark inevitability. The two halves of the painting mirror one another to the extent that, seen through half-closed eyes, they resemble shapes made by folding a piece of inked blotting paper in half.

This is apt, because the picture itself is a kind of hinge – a hinge on which the whole grand narrative of the ceiling turns. It is here that man sins, here that his fate is sealed. Adam and Eve break with God's commands and are separated from God for ever. Unity gives way to alienation, harmony gives way to discord, oneness becomes fragmentation. The three scenes that follow this one – all tracing the subsequent life of man on earth, through the story of Noah – are characterised by a busy brokenness, a mood of nightmare, a deliberate compositional disharmony, entirely at odds with the breadth and the sweeping simplicity that characterise the earlier scenes depicting the Creation. In this way, the very rhythms and formal structure of the paintings of the Sistine ceiling conspire to define mortal life – the life that follows the Fall – as disharmony, disconnection, alienation.

On the left, Adam and Eve are depicted as youthful, energetic figures. The semi-reclining Eve is flushed with excitement, antici-pation sparkling in her eyes, as she reaches round to take the fruit offered by the serpent – a creature depicted by Michelangelo as half-woman, half-snake, the long coils of its serpentine tail twined round the trunk of the tree. The face of the creature resembles those of the maenads and furies in ancient art. There is a resem-blance, too, to the face of Adam. The two figures have the same flowing yellow hair. Their gestures even seem to flow towards one another in a convergence of erotic energy.

The Fall of Man had often been interpreted as a surrender to impure desire, and its sexual aspect is strongly emphasised by

Michelangelo. The tree of knowledge bears not apples but figs, which have a traditional sexual significance. Eve kneels, not to pray, but to seduce. Her left hand is suggestively entwined in that of the serpent, from whose fist several fruit protrude. Adam reaches greedily, with a claw-like hand, towards a bunch of figs in the shadowy leaves next to the mouth of the snake-woman, while his own genitals hang like fruit beside the mouth of Eve. The middle finger of Eve's right hand is emphatically extended in a crude gesture and points down towards her own sex. Adam has turned into shadow, his face half-hidden in profile, to indicate that he has chosen the way of darkness. Eve's outstretched arm is rhymed by the shape of the dead tree stump against which she reclines, to show that in reaching towards temptation she has embraced the world of mortality and forsaken eternal life. Both are depicted against an outcrop of barren rock, another stark symbol of death.

In making Adam such an active figure, one who does not blindly follow Eve but vigorously reaches into the tree to pick the fruit himself, Michelangelo emphasises that the couple are implicated in a partnership of sin. The artist also stresses, by this means, that Adam has acted out of his own free will. Adam's energies are Promethean in their unruly vigour. He does not only reach into the tree but also pulls its main branch down towards him. The gesture that he makes with the arm closest to the serpent, both stretching out and groping for the figs with the index finger of his right hand, is a graceless parody of the gesture with which God brought him into being in *The Creation of Adam*. This is the moment in the narrative of the ceiling when man seeks to take control of his own destiny, when he sets out to become, as the guileful serpent suggests, a god himself. The result is disaster. God's pointing finger conjures life from nothing. But Adam, in reaching for divinity, conjures only the spectres of death and hardship, and condemns Man to a world of pain.

In suggesting the complexity of Adam and Eve's motives in this moment of Original Sin, Michelangelo indicates the multitude of evils encompassed within it – greed, treachery, God-defying insolence, a whole Pandora's box of ill intentions. John Milton, who retold the story of the Fall of Man a century later in his epic poem *Paradise Lost*, never saw *The Temptation and Expulsion*. But Milton's puritanically severe reflections on the nature of Original Sin, in a prose work entitled *De Doctrina Christiana*, set forth a view of the subject very close to that expressed in Michelangelo's painting:

> If the circumstances of this crime are duly considered, it will be acknowledged to have been a most heinous offence, and a transgression of the whole law. For what sin can be named, that was not included in this one act? It comprehended at once distrust in the divine veracity, and a proportionate credulity in the assurances of Satan; unbelief; ingratitude; disobedience; gluttony; in the man excessive uxoriousness, in the woman a want of proper regard for her husband, in both an insensibility for the welfare of their offspring, and that offspring the whole human race; parricide, theft, invasion of the rights of others, sacrilege, deceit, presumption in aspiring to divine attributes, fraud in the means employed to attain the object, pride, and arrogance . . .[6]

The other side of the painting, the bleak mirror image of Adam and Eve choosing sin, represents the moment of their punishment and belated remorse. An angel reaches out with a sword – a punitive gesture that rhymes cruelly with the enticing gesture of the serpent offering fruit – to expel the couple from the Garden of Eden. Adam's face is twisted into a rictus of anguish, and he looks instantly older and more wizened, as though mortality has already begun to work its effects on his flesh. Eve has metamorphosed into a hideous caricature of her former seductive self, a lumpen, lumbering being – a member of the same crude tribe of antediluvian giants that will soon be encountered, stumbling to their destruction, in Michelangelo's depiction of *The Deluge*.

As she takes her first steps into the world, the mother of mankind scowls and covers her breasts in shame, looking around over her shoulder, one last time, at paradise lost. She might be looking back at her own image beneath the tree, seeing the memory of the happy self she once was, but can never be again.

III

The Genesis Cycle, last triad: *The Deluge*;
The Sacrifice of Noah; *The Drunkenness of Noah*

The nine narrative paintings that span the vault of the Sistine Chapel climax in a catastrophic scene of universal destruction illustrating the events of *The Deluge*. Although it comes near the end of the sequence, it was the very first picture to be painted. The fresco is the largest of the three images in the cycle telling the story of Noah. Its theme is human sinfulness punished by the omnipotent Almighty, the moment when the vengeful and unpredictable God of the Old Testament 'saw that the wickedness of man was great in the earth, and that every imagination in the thoughts of his heart was only evil continually ... And the Lord said, I will destroy man whom I have created from the face of the earth; both man, and beast, and the creeping thing, and the fowls of the air; for it repenteth me that I have made them ...' (Genesis 6: 5–7).

Noah alone is exempt, for God finds that he is 'righteous'. He is told to build an ark from gopher wood, and to take on board all of his family. He must also give shelter to every species of animal, 'to keep seed alive on all the face of the earth', for God intends to send a great flood to cleanse the wicked world. As the waters rise, Noah and his family board the ark; 'the same day were all the fountains of the great deep broken up, and the windows of heaven were opened . . . And every living substance was destroyed which was upon the face of the ground . . .' (Genesis 7).

Michelangelo fleshed out this starkly told tale, transforming it into a panorama of human misery. A disjointed crowd of refugees seek their last haven in a drowning world. The floods of divine vengeance, which despite a raging tempest are not storm-tossed but eerily still, stretch to the horizon, forming a blue-grey field of watery nothingness that will, inexorably, engulf and erase all. In places, especially on the right-hand side of the composition, this dull-coloured void is so extensive that the artist might almost have left the fresco bare. This effect has been accidentally exaggerated by a patch of actual paint loss, caused by an explosion in the nearby Castel Sant'Angelo in 1797, which made a section of painted plaster fall to the ground. But a contrast between emptiness and fullness was, in any case, certainly part of Michelangelo's intention. It is an apt pictorial metaphor for his subject – which is, itself, a great unmaking. A vigorous crowd of the damned is being encroached upon by an expanse so blank as to be virtually abstract. Seen through half-closed eyes *The Deluge* resembles a picture that has been partly whitewashed. The world is a picture that God can unpaint at any moment.

Michelangelo envisages a moment when the flood has risen so high that only two mountainous outcrops protrude above the waters. To these precarious points of refuge the last remnants of humanity cling, as if washed up by the tides like so much flotsam and jetsam. On the right-hand side of the picture, a group of lamenting figures takes shelter beneath a makeshift tent strung between two tree trunks. To the left, a tribe of antediluvian humanity winds its way up towards the cramped, plateau-like summit of a mountain. Scale is hard to determine in this blasted, almost empty place, but the considerable height of these stunned unfortunates, measured against the single leafless tree that fails to offer them shelter, suggests they are beings of gargantuan stature. 'There were giants in the earth in those days; and also after that, when the sons of God came in unto the daughters of men, and they bear children to them, the same became mighty men, which were of old ...' (Genesis 6: 4). Forming a procession of the damned, these doomed titans concentrate on carrying their possessions – pots and pans, articles of clothing and furniture – to safety.

Michelangelo rarely descends to such detail, being one of the least circumstantial artists of the Italian Renaissance. His principal instrument of self-expression is the nude, on which he plays innumerable variations, the corollary of which is that as an artist he shows little interest in the mundane details of day-to-day existence. For him, painting and sculpture, like poetry, were essentially means by which spiritual ideas might be expressed. Francisco de Holanda, a Portuguese illuminator who made his acquaintance in Rome in the 1540s, recorded a conversation in which Michelangelo expressed a revealing level of disdain for the the oil painters of the Flemish tradition. 'They paint in Flanders,' he said to de Holanda, 'only to deceive the external eye, things that gladden you and of which you cannot speak ill. Their painting is of stuffs, bricks and mortar, the grass of the fields, the shadows of trees, and bridges and rivers, which they call landscapes, and little figures here and there. And all this, though it may appear good to some eyes, is in truth done without *reason*, without symmetry or proportion, without care in selecting or rejecting.' He added, dismissively, that such an art was capable of pleasing only 'young women, monks and nuns, or certain noble persons who have no ear for true harmony'.[7]

By Michelangelo's own stern standards, *The Deluge* pays an unparalleled degree of attention to the minutiae of ordinary life. At the back of the group of hapless figures hurrying uphill away from the waters, the artist includes an impassive woman in a simple turban. She balances an upturned kitchen stool on her head, on which are poised a conical clay soup jar – inventories reveal that Michelangelo's own kitchen contained a similar vessel – some loaves of unleavened bread, a stack of crockery, a knife and a spit for turning meat. Painted in muted tones of earth and off-white, this is the artist's only recorded still-life. The woman carrying it is preceded, in the headlong rush to safety, by two male figures who are similarly laden. The first, a youth whose long tresses of blond hair are blown sideways by the gale-force wind that courses through the whole scene, carries in his left hand a roll of salmon-pink cloth and a long-handled frying pan. The second bears a heavy bundle wrapped in a blanket, stooping under his load like Atlas carrying the world on his shoulders. On the island to the right, the group of sheltering figures has managed to salvage a keg of wine. One slumped and almost comatose figure, supported by two others, has clearly drunk deeply from it, in an attempt to anaesthetise himself from the terror of imminent death. Another fearful young man, his body curled up in a foetus-like position, lies across that same, presumably emptied, keg. Staring out across the waters with a blank-eyed expression, he seems petrified by fear.

Michelangelo draws attention to these small details but does so in a way devoid of all compassion. The objects that these people have stored against their ruin are not intended to evoke pathos; they are items of incriminatory evidence. These men and women are doomed precisely because they have taken too much pleasure in the things of this world, while paying too little heed to the state of their souls. The objects depicted are themselves pointedly symbolic. One group has loaves of bread; the other has wine. To Michelangelo's audience, bread and wine would inevitably have evoked the Eucharist, the mystical body of Christ consumed by the faithful during communion. But the bread and wine in *The Deluge* are unsanctified remains of impious feasts, symbolising the sins of an irredeemable multitude.

The painting contains numerous pointed inversions of this kind, parodies of the language of high and sacred art that serve to underline the cursed state of this antediluvian multitude. The naked young man curled against the wine keg resembles a Roman river god – in antique art, the gods of the rivers were conventionally depicted leaning on upturned, gushing water vessels. But instead of presiding over a life-giving flow of water, Michelangelo's youth prepares to die a watery death. The reclining woman in the other group, to the far left of the composition, also resembles a Roman river deity. But she too is a symbol of death and aridity, rather than fertile life. Her breasts are empty and will bear no more milk, as the weeping infant at her shoulder makes clear.

This pattern of inversion is carried through to several other figures to the left of the painting, which seem calculated to evoke sacred associations, only for those associations to be simultaneously denied. A young man bearing his wife on his back recalls St Christopher carrying the Christ child across the waters. A young woman, who is haloed by a wind-blown arc of plum-coloured drapery, and who holds her smiling and oblivious baby close to her, calls to mind innumerable images of the Madonna and Child. A group truncated by the edge of the frame, to the extreme left, includes another woman with a baby, next to whom patiently stands a donkey – imagery that evokes the Holy Family's rest on the flight to Egypt. But there is to be no rest for these people, no blessing, no salvation. Michelangelo takes a particular and even cruel relish in forcing the message home, by filling his work with such echoes of other, happier themes. He imparts a brutish, crude quality to these figures, that makes them seem both primitive and irredeemably earthbound. The standing mother is confirmed as an anti-Madonna by the set, sullen, stupid expression on her face. Not one of the doomed titans looks up, or makes time to pray.

Michelangelo was personally inclined to asceticism, to the point of flaunting his own frugality. His letters home to Florence, to the family whom he subsidised (despite their pretensions to high social rank), are peppered with self-righteous references to the poverty of his own existence. Giorgio Vasari, in his life of Michelangelo, remarks both on the simplicity of his clothes and on his reluctance to change them. 'In his latter years he wore buskins of dogskin on the legs, next to the skin, constantly for whole months together, so that afterwards, when he came to take them off, on drawing them off the skin often came away with them. Over the stockings he wore boots of cordwain fastened on the inside, as a protection against the damp.'[8]

Ascanio Condivi, in his own biography of Michelangelo – much of which was probably written under dictation from the artist himself – stresses that he often worked so hard that he went without food and sleep. Condivi also links Michelangelo's religious thought to that of the most notoriously ascetic preacher of the late fifteenth century, Girolamo Savonarola (1452–98). In

Condivi's words, the artist 'read the Holy Scriptures with great application and study, both the Old Testament and the New, as well as the writings of those who have studied them, such as Savonarola, for whom he has always had great affection and whose voice still lives in his memory'.[9]

Michelangelo's older brother, Leonardo, had become a member of the Dominican order and a follower of Savonarola when the artist was sixteen years old. Michelangelo clearly harboured vivid memories of the sermons with which Savonarola had electrified the population of Florence in the late 1480s and 1490s – apocalyptic prophecies of doom that had urged the people of the city into orgies of mass repentance. 'Rethink you well, O ye rich, for affliction shall smite ye,' Savonarola had preached, in one of his many hellfire sermons. 'This city shall no more be Florence, but a den of thieves, of turpitude and bloodshed. Then shall ye all be poverty-stricken, all wretched, and your name, O priests, shall be changed into a terror ... know that unheard-of times are at hand.' Savonarola's followers, known as the Weepers – *i Piagnoni* – piled their worldly possessions into 'bonfires of the vanities', burning books, 'lascivious paintings' and other such symbols of luxury and decadence. *The Deluge* is a picture shadowed by the apocalyptic terrors conjured up by Savonarola's sermons. Those who have clung on to the vanities of this worldly life are receiving their punishment – not by fire but by water.

In 1494, Savonarola had delivered the most famous of all his series of sermons, on the theme of Noah's Ark. He had prophesied a second flood, a prediction soon fulfilled, at least in the lively metaphorical imaginings of his Florentine followers, in the form of the invading armies of France, led by King Charles VIII. The preacher had warned his listeners to pray and take refuge in Florence cathedral, which he compared to the mystical Ark of

Christ's mercy. In comparing the redemptive role of the Ark to that of Christ, Savonarola was drawing on a long tradition of Christian allegory, in which the stories of the Old Testament were recast as prophetic prefigurations of the teachings of the New. In the allegorical exegeses of the Old Testament expounded by medieval theologians, Noah had always been treated as one of the precursors of the Saviour. The waters of the flood were compared to the purifying waters of baptism, the wood of the Ark to the wood of the cross, and the door in the Ark to the wound in Christ's side.

Such ideas had determined the conventions for depicting the story of Noah for many centuries. For generations the Ark itself – representing, as in Savonarola's rhetoric, the Christian Church afloat in the sea of the world – dominated most depictions of the subject of the Deluge. By contrast, Michelangelo gives it relatively scant pictorial prominence, making it little more than a background detail – although he does give it symbolic weight, by placing it directly between his two refuges of the doomed. He paints it very much as a metaphor for the Church, making it resemble a religious building more than a boat. Under siege from a desperate group of antediluvian giants equipped with a ladder, it remains impregnable, a fortress of true faith. Oblivious to the fracas taking place below him, Noah leans out of an upper window to salute the heavens.

The building Michelangelo's Ark most closely resembles is none other than the heavily fortified Sistine Chapel itself; and it is tempting to suppose that the artist, as he painted the great vault of the chapel, may even have felt a sense of kinship with Noah. Michelangelo too was a man far above the teeming multitude, doing his best to serve God's obscure purpose and follow the path of righteousness. A solitary individual, he had a barely concealed contempt for the herd-like masses (such as the young women, monks, nuns and tasteless rich whom he lumped together in his diatribe on Flemish art). He may well have thought of the Sistine Chapel – the isolation chamber in which he lived, and worked, for almost four years – as his own Ark. Looked at from beneath, the wooden scaffold that he had devised for painting the ceiling – a series of arches on cantilevers wedged into holes drilled above the cornice, each one supporting a painting deck – must have somewhat resembled an upturned boat.

The Deluge was a profoundly original painting, however, precisely because Michelangelo relegated the Ark to the background – something no artist before him had done. He had decided to tell his story principally through the depiction of a crowd of struggling humanity. A convulsive, intermittent energy courses through the whole scene. This rhythm of anguish and despair connects the outstretched arms of the woman and the bearded patriarch on the island to the angular boughs and branches of the blasted tree on the other side, which itself resembles a hand desperately reaching out for help. These energies reach a pitch in the flat-bottomed boat at the centre of the composition, where fighting has broken out between those already embarked, in a desperate attempt to reach the Ark, and those wanting to climb on board to save themselves. Here all the desperation of the story is distilled to a series of violent, doomed struggles taking place in a watery void.

When Michelangelo painted this scene, he may well have had in mind Dante's description of travelling to the cursed City of Dis, in the eighth canto of the *Inferno*, in which the poet finds himself on a boat that is attacked by would-be boarders from the depths of a river of the damned. Three centuries later, when the French Romantic Eugène Delacroix painted a celebrated picture inspired by that same passage from Dante, to which he gave the title *The Barque of Dante*, it was to the example of Michelangelo's boatload of the doomed that he would turn for visual inspiration. Delacroix sensed intuitively the kinship that existed between Dante and Michelangelo, and recognised that it was particularly strong in *The Deluge*. Michelangelo admired Dante more than any other Italian writer. His vision of the flood is a Dantean vision of hell, realised in painting rather than poetry.

'Is disproportion one of the conditions that compel admiration?' Delacroix asked this rhetorical question in his journal entry of 8 May 1853. He had Michelangelo on his mind again: 'If Mozart, Cimarosa and Racine are less striking because of the perfect proportion in their works, do not Shakespeare, Michelangelo and Beethoven owe something of their effect to the opposite quality?'[10] Once more, the French painter may have been thinking of *The Deluge*, a picture long regarded as a great example of Michelangelo's sublime irregularity. It is one of the most vigorously muscular of all his compositions, but it could hardly be described as a work of perfect proportion. It is singularly lacking in pictorial grace and harmony – a discordant, fragmented creation, which is almost impossible to contemplate as a unified whole. The multitude of figures within it can easily appear, to the eye straining upward to discern the logic of their organisation, like separate groups of sculptures on display in a museum.

The conventional explanation for this is that Michelangelo was still grappling with the challenge of painting the chapel's immense ceiling when he planned the composition of *The Deluge*. According to this frequently repeated argument, he made a fatal misjudgement of scale, overloading the work with such a surfeit of figures as to make it barely legible from the floor of the chapel beneath – a mistake that he did not repeat when he painted the other narrative works, in which the figures are both fewer and more monumental in scale.

But such a view involves a serious misreading of the coherence of the Sistine Chapel ceiling as a whole. The cycle of frescoes begins with the creation of the universe, of the world and of man within it. It hymns the immeasurable, illimitable unity of God the Creator and celebrates the moment when the spark of life is imparted to Adam, the first of men. Henceforth, its rhythms implacably express the view of human existence implicit in the story of the Fall. Unity with God becomes disunity and separation. As Man departs Eden and enters the world of history, the human race both multiplies and fragments, taking on a myriad of forms – all of which represent, from different angles, so to speak, the condition of having fallen from grace. This process reaches its climax in *The Deluge*. The disconnected figures thronging the picture look like leaves scattered in the wind by comparison with the more monumental figures on the ceiling, such as God the Creator or the languorous Adam. But that is no error on the part of Michelangelo. It is a device that exactly expresses the severe world view of the Old Testament.

That severity is, however, tempered by a significant detail. Two figures are set apart from the rest in *The Deluge*: an aged father struggling to support the body of his dead son. These are the only figures calculated to evoke genuine sympathy, and the only ones who seem tragic rather than merely unregenerate. They are also unique in that they alone elicit a sympathetic response from those around them.

Placed in isolation near the centre of the painting, this group may have been intended as a symbol of hope, an allusion to the future coming of Christ, and the redemption of mankind. The old man recalls Joseph or Nicodemus lowering the body of Christ from the Cross in scenes of the Deposition. The association was certainly made by the artist himself. Much later in life, Michelangelo would adapt this same group to create a number of images of Christ in the arms of Nicodemus. The most famous of these is the celebrated late sculpture of the *Pietà* now in Florence's Museo del Duomo, in which he gave the anguished Nicodemus his own face as an old man (see p. 172).

It is part of Michelangelo's unruly greatness as an artist that the meanings of his work cannot be easily confined. It is impossible to say exactly what he intended by including that statuesque father bearing his dead son through the blasted world of *The Deluge*. But it is an image that complicates this otherwise ruthlessly ascetic, apocalyptic vision of sinful humanity punished by the God of Genesis. It does so by introducing into it a pathos and ambiguity that amount, themselves, to a lament on behalf of suffering humanity. Life is pain and life is mystery. Faith may be the only path but it is not an easy one. The sons of Adam must suffer the inscrutability of their God, like powerless children.

★   ★   ★

The Deluge is flanked by two other paintings representing scenes from the biblical story of Noah. The first of these, which can be identified as *The Sacrifice of Noah*, appears to be the only one of the Sistine ceiling's narrative pictures to have been placed out of chronological sequence. It precedes *The Deluge*, although logic dictates that it should come afterwards, given that its subject is Noah's sacrifice to God for having spared him and his family from the Flood. The subject is described in Genesis 8: 20–1: 'And Noah builded an altar unto the Lord; and took of every clean beast, and of every clean fowl, and offered burnt offerings on the altar. And the Lord smelled a sweet savour; and the Lord said in his heart, I will not again curse the ground any more for man's sake; for the imagination of man's heart is evil from his youth; neither will I again smite any more everything living, as I have done.'

Michelangelo's decision to place this scene first has been the cause of some confusion. The artist's early biographers, Giorgio Vasari and Ascanio Condivi, assumed that the picture did not illustrate the life of Noah at all, but must represent the sacrifice of Cain and Abel. Their explanation, which has been followed by some modern scholars, has the virtue of restoring chronological integrity to Michelangelo's fresco cycle (since Cain and Abel's sacrifice occurs well before the Flood in the Book of Genesis). But it is contradicted by the visual evidence of the fresco itself. There are no obvious candidates for the figures of Cain and Abel, while Abel's offering, 'the fruit of the ground' (Genesis 4: 3), is nowhere to be seen. The congested queue of animals awaiting sacrifice, which include an elephant, is surely intended to suggest the multitude of living creatures disgorged from the Ark.

Comparison with the other frescoes definitively confirms the subject as *The Sacrifice of Noah*. The patriarch may only appear as a diminutive figure in *The Deluge*, but his principal attributes are unmistakable. He wears red, and he has a long white beard. So too does the figure at the centre of Michelangelo's scene of sacrifice. The altar over which he presides stands next to a structure resembling part of the Ark in *The Deluge*. There is further supporting evidence, if any were needed, in the distinct similarity between Noah's three sons in the nearby *Drunkenness of Noah* and three of the youths assisting at the rite in *The Sacrifice* – the boy bearing logs for the fire, the boy kneeling astride the dead ram, and the boy peering into the altar flames. They are the same figures in different poses.

So the chronological conundrum remains, but Michelangelo's apparently puzzling decision to place the scene out of sequence is most plausibly explained as a victory for expressive power over strict narrative coherence. *The Deluge*, a subject that involved multitudes fleeing a rising flood, clearly called out for the largest of the three fields dictated by the structure of the ceiling's design. The artist must have been reluctant to relegate it to the first of his two smaller panels, so, instead, he placed *The Sacrifice* there.

Michelangelo was the first artist of the Italian Renaissance to create an image of *The Sacrifice of Noah* that evokes the pagan sacrifices depicted on sarcophagi and other works of antique art. His predecessors, such as Jacopo della Quercia, who had depicted the life of Noah in his bas-reliefs on the doors of San Petronio in Bologna, represented the episode as a comparatively inert act of devotion, showing the patriarch and his family joined in prayer around a simple altar – a far cry from Michelangelo's dynamic frieze of turning, twisting figures.

In deciding to treat the subject in this way, Michelangelo was looking back in time, past the early Renaissance and the Middle Ages to the distant traditions of Greece and Rome. The artists of antiquity had dwelt in much detail on the material preparations for acts of sacrifice to their many gods – the preparation of offerings, the lighting of fires – and Michelangelo drew direct inspiration from such classical sources in planning his own com-position. Noah's daughter-in-law, who shields her face from the heat as she places a brand of wood in the sacrificial fire, is directly derived from a figure representing Althea in a frieze on a Roman sarcophagus. The youth seen from behind, crouching to peer into the flames, may have been based in part on a similar figure on a sarcophagus in the museum of antiquities at Naples. He bears an even closer resemblance to the lower, struggling figure in one of the most celebrated surviving classical statues, the pair of marble wrestlers preserved in the Uffizi Galleries at Florence. Since this work was only excavated in 1583, Michelangelo cannot have known it directly. But it seems probable that he was familiar with a similar sculpture, subsequently lost to the ravages of time.

Michelangelo's allusions to classical sculpture should not be taken to signal an unthinking admiration for the world of antiquity. The opposite is the case. On this occasion, he uses the figural language of Roman art, with its straining, busy forms, to suggest that Noah's children are so wrapped up in the bloody acts of animal sacrifice that they misunderstand the true significance of the rite in which they partake – the implication being that they are almost as lost in ignorance as those devotees of ancient pagan cults whom the artist has made them resemble. They wrestle with the reluctant beasts; they carry wood; they tend the fire and exchange a bloody parcel of viscera, destined for the flames. The contrast between these figures and that of Noah himself could hardly be more extreme. While they are lost in mere action, he is absorbed in solemn contemplation. His eyes are lowered, his head bowed in thought. Those around him resemble warriors, but he looks like a priest. His shaven head even faintly resembles a priest's tonsure.

In the contrast between Noah's stillness and the movement all around him lies the essence of the picture. In the theology of Michelangelo's time Noah's offering was seen as a prefiguration of the Mass, the salvific re-enactment of Christ's death, the offering of his flesh and blood as bread and wine. It is to that higher rite that Noah's gesture, pointing heavenwards, prophetically refers. A stark contrast is drawn between the old rites of sacrifice, made redundant by the coming of Christ, and the pure rite of the Mass – between the acceptable and the unacceptable offering.

It is a characteristically Michelangelesque image, nonetheless, one that places a single, inspired individual in a pit of fools. The solemn, white-bearded prophet, rapt in contemplation of the true spirit of God, is surrounded by a crowd of the unenlightened, whirled in the circle of their own restless energies around a vortex of flames.

★   ★   ★

The last painting in the final triad of the ceiling's narrative frescoes is *The Drunkenness of Noah*. The picture is a lesson in human frailty, and a meditation on the mysterious workings of God. At first glance it might appear to be one of the most backward-looking of Michelangelo's compositions. But in fact it is a highly inventive, unusual picture, pregnant with possibility for future generations of artists.

As in the narrative paintings of the Middle Ages and early Renaissance, the painting breaks with the unities of time, place and action to tell its story like a comic strip, with the same protagonist shown in two different situations at two different moments in time. To the left, the red-robed Noah sets to with his spade, working the land that God has spared from the Flood, and has blessed with fertility: 'And Noah began to be an husbandman; and he planted a vineyard' (Genesis 9: 20). He is silhouetted against a harsh white sky and confronted with an expanse of yellow ochre ground that seems so harsh and desert-like that his spade barely penetrates its surface. In this particular passage of the painting, Michelangelo proposes an image as simple and emblematic as a piece of heraldry, as schematic as the *impresa* on a Renaissance shield or flag – a rugged symbol of the lot of man after the Fall, doomed to a life of hard labour.

To the right, Noah appears again. But this time he is naked, no longer the righteous patriarch but an all too mortal man, who has indulged too much in the wine that his vineyard has produced: 'And he drank of the wine, and was drunken; and he was uncovered within his tent' (Genesis 9: 21). He reclines in a stupor, his head sunk upon his chest. He appears as another of Michelangelo's parodies of the figure of an ancient Roman river god, like the petrified boy hunched over the wine cask in *The Deluge*. His sons, Ham, Shem and Japheth, shocked by the sudden apparition of their inebriated father, gesticulate and prepare to cover his nakedness.

This troubling, dreamlike picture is susceptible to different levels of interpretation. Within traditional Christian theology, its message was one of hope, since throughout the Middle Ages and the Renaissance this episode was seen as one among many Old Testament stories in which was prophesied – as through a glass, darkly – the redemptive sacrifice of Christ. Like Christ, Noah was stripped bare and humiliated in the eyes of mankind. The torpor of Noah's drunkenness was, symbolically, a small death, foreshadowing the death of Christ on the Cross. Noah's drunkenness was also held to prefigure Christ's Passion, in that while Noah seeded the vine and drank of its fruit, Christ said, 'I am the true vine, and my Father is the husbandman' (John 15: 1) – a sacrifice commemorated daily at Mass, in the wine of the Eucharist. Michelangelo reinforces those ancient associations by placing a pitcher at the end of the hard wooden bed on which Noah has collapsed. A clay wine cup is at his side, as if to suggest the blood that will course from the wound in Christ's side when he is crucified on the Cross. This allusion would not have been lost on Michelangelo's contemporaries, familiar as they were with images of the Crucifixion in which angels descend from heaven, bearing goblets in which to catch the precious drops seeping from Christ's wounds (a well-known example is the so-called *Mond Crucifixion* in the National Gallery, painted by Michelangelo's contemporary Raphael).

Yet Michelangelo complicates his vision of *The Drunkenness of Noah*, adding and inventing elements that are entirely his own to impart a deeper structure of meanings to the scene. The broader pattern of images on the Sistine Chapel ceiling, which creates an interlocking network of symbols and allusions – like themes repeated and varied in musical composition – instantly imparts a dark and penitential note to this image of an unregenerate drunkard shamed before his sons. Joel, the prophet enthroned immediately to the left of the scene, had railed against the sinfulness of those who fall into inebriation: 'Awake, ye drunkards, and weep; and howl all ye drinkers of wine' (Joel 1: 5). Moreover, the all-encompassing symmetry of the nine narrative panels on the main vault invites the viewer to see *The Drunkenness of Noah*, the very last image, as a pair with the very first, *The Separation of Light and Darkness*. The contrast is striking and severe, its effect like that of a scything caesura in poetry. On one side, the all-powerful God reaches up with a majestic gesture to bring light from the darkness – and, by implication, to wrestle good from evil; on the other, a mere man lies slumped ignominiously in the den of his own sinfulness, impelled, despite himself, to repeat the error of Adam's Fall.

The Drunkenness of Noah is a work that shows how deeply Michelangelo responded to the compressed, laconic and enigmatic style of Old Testament epic. The artist may not be inclined to dwell on the particularities of specific human emotions – he stands, in this regard, at the opposite end of the spectrum to a painter such as Rembrandt, or a sculptor such as Donatello – yet he has his own deep sense of humanity. In painting the Sistine Chapel ceiling, Michelangelo did not only reflect on the Book of Genesis, digest its meanings and ponder the detail of its stories. He expressed, with terrible poignancy, the predicament of those who are created and controlled by the veiled God of the ancient Hebraic tradition. They live under the perpetual threat of self-alienation and cannot help becoming other than they once were.

It is the lot of every great figure of the Old Testament, from Adam onwards, to follow God's will and to embody his purposes as best they can, but in doing so they often find themselves terrifyingly helpless – uniquely helpless, by comparison with the heroes encountered in any of the world's other epic literary traditions. The God of the Old Testament not only sends them challenges and trials of unfathomable mystery (the instruction to Abraham to sacrifice his son Isaac; the myriad ills heaped on the head of Job). He also changes them, within themselves, within their very beings, in ways that are equally beyond their comprehension and power to predict.

This aspect of the Old Testament stories was perceptively analysed by the German literary critic Eric Auerbach in an essay entitled 'Odysseus's Scar'.[11] Auerbach, whose method was comparative, believed the particular qualities of biblical narrative were thrown into sharp relief by the counter-example of Greek epic. In particular, he drew a series of telling contrasts between the heroes of the Hebraic tradition and those of the Homeric legends. The heroes of Homer, he noted, change little. They are people whose 'destiny is clearly defined and who wake every morning as though it were the first day of their lives: their emotions, though strong, are simple and find expression instantly'. But those who play their part in the stories of the Old Testament are different. They are more inward and variable, more cloaked, even to themselves. They are separated in time and place, horizontally distant from one another but joined by their vertical connection to God – a God whom they know they must serve, but whose purposes are hidden from them. Life, for them, is the painful process of discovering what lies in store. 'The stern hand of God is ever upon the Old Testament figures; he has not only made them once and for all and chosen them, but he continues to work upon them, bends them and kneads them, and, without destroying them in essence, produces from them forms which their youth gave no grounds for anticipating.'

This is Michelangelo's theme in *The Drunkenness of Noah*. An Old Testament hero succumbs to a great transformation, realised in the forms and colours of a vivid nightmare. The artist has created an image that seems to externalise the hero's awareness of his own complexity – making visible, so to speak, the dark thoughts that are present only as a shadow across the face of his carved *David*. Noah could be dreaming the scene of his own humiliation, such is the hallucinogenic power of Michelangelo's representation of the scene. The artist paints it as a phantasmagoria, lends it a quality of inward vision found nowhere else in the world of his time, save perhaps in that hauntingly weird fifteenth-century prose romance, the *Hypnerotomachia Poliphili*, a work of fiction by the Dominican friar Francesco Colonna, quite probably known to Michelangelo, in which the hero progresses through a landscape of architectural and sculptural dream imagery that feels like a projection of his own thoughts and fantasies.

Once more, the depth of Michelangelo's originality can be measured by the extent to which he departed both from the literal Genesis narrative and from established visual convention. Earlier artists had shown Noah drunk among his vines, which they usually imagined as a form of leafy arbour. By contrast, Michelangelo places him inside a wooden shed so dark it might be a cellar. Objects in this space assume the characteristics of things seen in dreams, being either over-scaled or unnaturally clear and distinct from one another. The wine vat behind Noah looms ominously while the bowl and pitcher beside him are held in a light that gives them a trembling, oneiric particularity. These are effects that anticipate, by some five hundred years, those found in the 'metaphysical' paintings of Giorgio de' Chirico and the dreamlike art of the Surrealists.

In the Book of Genesis, Noah is discovered in his drunken state by his son Ham, who fetches his brothers Shem and Japheth: 'And Shem and Japheth took a garment, and laid it upon both their shoulders, and went backward, and covered the nakedness of their father; and their faces were backward, and they saw not their father's nakedness.' But in Michelangelo's painting, these relationships are all changed. The three sons confront their father's nakedness together. None faces backward and none is allowed to escape the shock of the encounter.

The sight of their father is like an apparition, an image from out of the dark. As Charles de Tolnay noted, Noah is 'like a marble statue placed on a temporary wooden base'.[12] He might almost be a sculpture that they have excavated from the ground – like the antique sculpture of the struggling Laocoön and his sons, doomed by the Greek gods to die wrapped in the coils of serpents, that Michelangelo himself had witnessed being excavated in Rome in January 1506, two years before he painted this picture. The memory of the *Laocoön*, a work that made a deep and lasting impression on Michelangelo, seems embedded in this painting, which also joins a father with his sons in a moment of crisis and pain. Even the draperies that play about the figures have a writhing, serpentine quality.

Whereas the Bible implies that Noah's sons themselves are clothed – which was how earlier artists had envisaged the scene – Michelangelo paints them as nudes, just like their father, giving them merely token robes that do nothing to obscure them. This is a daring invention, epitomising his bold habit of transforming the conventions of religious art, bending them to purposes and meanings that evade purely theological analysis. The young men's upright, athletic and muscular bodies, lit by an irregular play of lights and darks, as though by the flare of lamplight, contrast cruelly with Noah's slack and slumped form. The image is an archetype of that moment, late in the father–son relationship, when the child must take on the role of parent because the parent, enfeebled, has become a kind of child. It can also be seen as a metaphor for the sudden, shocking recognition of death as an ineluctable fact of human existence.

Seeing their father like this confronts the sons with their own mortality and mutability – that mutability which, within the scheme of the Old Testament stories, governs all of life in the postlapsarian world. As he is now, so they will become. Their powerlessness to change that fact is emphasised by the inadequate flimsiness of the wisp-like drapery with which they have been furnished. The sons cannot cover their father's shame and they reflect his vulnerability in their own uncovered state. Man is always naked before God.

IV

The Four Spandrel Paintings: *David and Goliath*; *Judith and Holofernes*; *The Death of Haman*; *The Brazen Serpent*

There are four spandrels, triangular in shape and curved in form, at the four corners of the ceiling. Michelangelo chose to decorate these awkward spaces with four more scenes from the Old Testament, creating a subordinate level of narrative below his story of the origins of the world and of human existence. They all depict episodes in which the people of Israel are miraculously saved from evil, or persecution, or their own weakness. The first two show *David and Goliath* and *Judith and Holofernes*. The subjects of the second pair are *The Death of Haman* and *The Brazen Serpent*. Each of these scenes of salvation, in accordance with the general pattern of the ceiling's meanings, is to be regarded as a prefiguration of the saving of all mankind by Jesus Christ. The four paintings also serve to unify the many disparate images in the whole lower zone of the vault, to which they belong – images of the prophets and the sibyls and the ancestors of Christ. As stories of Israel's salvation, they bear witness to God's perpetual presence in the life of all his people, and the constant renewal of the promise of redemption.

The four spandrel paintings bear witness to the tremendous evolution that occurred in Michelangelo's style between 1508, when he started the ceiling, and 1512, when he completed it. The first two were painted at the start of the project, the last two at its close. They might almost have been painted by different artists. So great is the difference between them that they demonstrate, more clearly than any other works on the vault, the extent to which Michelangelo had to wrestle his own mutating style into subordination to the totality of his scheme. The final two spandrel paintings are works of unique originality and virtuosity, even by the already extraordinary standards of the Sistine Chapel ceiling. They inaugurated a new style in Italian art that would eventually come to be known as *maniera*, or Mannerism – tense, nervy, difficult, violent. It is no surprise that Giorgio Vasari, who was himself a Mannerist – albeit of meagre talent – thought these paintings the finest on the whole vault.

The first two spandrel paintings are comparatively straightforward narrative images. They have a solid, grounded, earthbound quality. Each shows a single, frozen moment of drama.

David and Goliath represents the climax of the famous story told in the Book of Samuel. The Philistine army advanced upon Israel and a challenge was set. One man from each side would be chosen to represent his nation in a fight to the death. The champion of the Philistines was a man named Goliath of Gath, 'whose height was six cubits and a span' and who was armed with sword and shield, and a spear so large it 'was like a weaver's beam' (I Samuel 17: 4–7). The young hero David volunteered to fight for the Israelites, confident that the Lord would deliver him 'out of the hand of this Philistine'. Refusing arms and armour, 'he took his staff in his hand, and chose him five smooth stones out of the brook, and put them in a shepherd's bag which he had'. Running to meet Goliath, he let loose a stone from the sling 'and smote the Philistine in his forehead, that the stone sunk into his forehead; and he fell upon his face to the earth'. Having no sword, he quickly drew Goliath's own sword from its sheath, 'and slew him, and cut off his head therewith' (I Samuel 17: 32–51).

This is the moment that Michelangelo has depicted. The triumphant David, whose slingshot lies on the brown earth in the foreground, straddles the back of his fallen opponent. As Goliath struggles confusedly to rise to his feet, David seizes him by the hair and raises a scimitar aloft. The hero of the Israelites is solemnly focused on the task of beheading his opponent. There is no sense of exultation in his severe expression and the action is poised in a way that speaks of steady inevitability, of the divine will being done. The scene is set against the backdrop of the Philistine encampment, abbreviated by the artist to a pair of skulking faces at the base of a single pink and yellow tent. Its apex is cut off by the upper edge of the triangular spandrel. The shape of the sword raised in David's hand is perfectly silhouetted against the narrow band of yellow that stripes the upper part of the tent, and thus starkly isolated – a symbol of divine retribution against the wicked. Michelangelo has arranged the colour scheme of his composition in such a way that David's costume of blue, with a yellow cape, seems like a brighter version of Goliath's muted, sea-green cuirass with yellow trim. Both figures have hair that grows in tight curls, so that they might almost be larger and smaller versions of the same person. Good triumphs over evil, but Michelangelo's symmetry implies that the conflict between virtue and vice also represents, for every individual, an inner choice. In slaying Goliath, David is also, symbolically, subduing his own unruly passions.

The spandrel of *David and Goliath* is paired with that of *Judith and Holofernes*, which tells the story of how a beautiful and chaste Jewish heroine saved her people by slaying the general of the Assyrians. The tale is told in the Book of Judith, a text excluded from the Old Testament in Protestant translations, but still to be found in Orthodox and Roman Catholic bibles. Judith was a pious and beautiful woman, in mourning for her dead husband. She dressed plainly and spent all day praying and studying the Torah. When the Assyrians laid siege to her home town of Bethulia, Judith conceived a plan to save her people. She dressed in her finest clothes and went to the Assyrian camp, where she fooled her enemies into believing she wished to defect to their side. Holofernes, the Assyrian general, made advances to her and she agreed to have supper with him in his tent. While he gorged himself on many delicacies and wine, she ate only the humble kosher food that she had brought with her in a bag from Bethulia. When Holofernes fell into a deep, drunken slumber, she took his sword and beheaded him with it. She put his head in the bag that had held her provisions and escaped from the city. Michelangelo painted Judith leaving the tent, entrusting the severed head of the tyrant to her maidservant and looking back, one last time, at the corpse of her enemy.

It had been traditional to find a parallel between the stories of David and Goliath and Judith and Holofernes since the Middle Ages. Both are tales of the strong brought low by the weak, of evil conquered by good, with the help of God. For centuries it had also been conventional to interpret the stories as allegories of the triumph of particular virtues over particular vices. David's defeat of Goliath was seen as the victory of Fortitude over Greed. Judith's defeat of Holofernes was seen as the victory of Humility over Pride and Luxury. Such traditional distinctions were not absolute – Savonarola, for example, associated David instead with Humility – but they underpin Michelangelo's interpretation of the stories in the Sistine Chapel spandrels.

Just as the figure of David, stern and resolute, is the embodiment of fortitude, so Judith embodies humility. She is dressed in the fine clothes required by her stratagem, their colours echoing those of the clothes worn by David in the other spandrel. Under a greenish-white dress she wears a light blue bodice with a golden yellow border, as well as a headdress of matching blue and gold. As her maid stoops to allow Judith to cover the head of Holofernes with a cloth, the two figures, mirroring one another in graceful *contrapposto*, might almost be dancing. The head of the Assyrian general has been placed in a serving dish rather than the bag described in the Bible. Michelangelo may have chosen this detail by analogy with medieval and Renaissance depictions of another story from the Bible, in which John the Baptist's severed head is presented to Salome on a plate. Perhaps the artist felt that it would look undignified to have Judith cramming Holofernes's head into a sack, like a thief in the night. Putting the head on a dish is a more elegant solution, which also has the effect of emphasising Judith's humble, lowly status. She and her maid might be serving women removing the plates from a banquet.

The poorly preserved figure of a soldier slumbers at the edge of the scene. Judith looks as though she is walking on tiptoe, so as not to rouse the camp. She looks back into the darkness of Holofernes's tent, which Michelangelo has painted as a marble building, perhaps to emphasise the tyrant's association with luxury and decadence. Within that dark space, framed by curtains the colour of blood, the nightmare from which she has delivered her people still restlessly lurks. Sprawled on a rumpled white bedsheet, the decapitated body of Holofernes jerks menacingly, even in the last spasm of death. With his right hand the tyrant reaches above and behind him, as though sightlessly groping for the sword with which he has been decapitated. It has sometimes been believed that Michelangelo included his own likeness in the form of the tyrant's severed head. There is a faint resemblance to the artist as he became in his later years, but since he was only in his early thirties when painting the Sistine Chapel the idea that the wizened, bearded face of Holofernes really is a self-portrait seems fanciful.

★   ★   ★

Each of the first pair of spandrels depicts a single moment in time, whereas the later pair compress a multitude of incidents into their congested and convoluted compositions. Their subjects, linked once more by the theme of Israel's salvation, are *The Death of Haman* and *The Brazen Serpent*. In these works, Michelangelo leaves the still and solid world inhabited by Judith and David far behind. Each of the later spandrels is a phantasmagoria, filled with writhing, struggling figures, lit by fickle dapplings of glare. Their colours are acid and disjunct, a riot of sharp yellows and lime greens, of orange and gold, lilac and lavender. Whatever their intended place within the scheme of the ceiling, these are pictures of such eruptive, irregular, expressive force that they go beyond the meanings of their iconography. Symbolism of the type that can readily be applied to the earlier spandrel images of David and of Judith seems quite inadequate as a guide to these works. They give no strong sense of exemplifying any particular virtues and are shot through with a sense of agitation so extreme that it borders on hysteria.

The Death of Haman is drawn from a story in the Old Testament Book of Esther which defies succinct synopsis. Haman is chief minister to Ahasuerus, king of the Persians. His mortal enemy is Mordecai, a Jew serving in the chancellery, who has won royal favour in the past by foiling a plot hatched by two court chamberlains to assassinate the king. Mordecai has offended Haman by refusing to bow down to him as a mark of respect on his appointment as chief minister. To take his revenge, Haman plans to kill all the Jews in the Persian Empire. Mordecai learns of the plot and warns his cousin Esther, Ahasuerus's queen. Risking her life by appearing unbidden, she approaches the king, who offers to grant her anything she desires. Esther declines to tell Ahasuerus her wish but invites him, instead, to a banquet she has prepared for him and Haman. When the three meet, she once again demurs but tells the king that all will be revealed at a second banquet that she is preparing for him and Haman for the following day. Meanwhile, Haman, unaware of Esther's machinations against him, orders a great gallows to be constructed, from which he intends to have Mordecai hanged. That night the chronicles are read to Ahasuerus in his bedroom, reminding him of his old debt to Mordecai for saving his life. The next day, at the second banquet, Esther reveals to Ahasuerus that she is Jewish. She tells him of Haman's plans for a genocide of the Jews and begs the king to save her people. Soon after this, Haman vengefully attempts to rape Esther, is discovered by the king, and condemned to death. Ahasuerus decrees that he is to be hanged on the same gallows prepared for Mordecai. The king's will is done, Haman dies and the Jews are saved.

In squeezing a number of episodes from this breathlessly complicated narrative into the triangular shape of a single spandrel, Michelangelo created a busy and restless image, one so crowded that it is difficult to interpret with any great degree of certainty.

To the left, at least, there is no ambiguity. Here Michelangelo shows the second banquet, at which Esther tells Ahasuerus of Haman's plot. The king looks dumbfounded, while Haman reels away in surprise. In the middle, Haman meets his unpleasant end. To the right, matters are more complicated. Here, some kind of compressed version of the start of the tale appears to be illustrated, against the normal convention of narrative chronology unfolding from left to right. At the threshold of the palace, Mordecai, dressed in yellow, urgently gestures to Esther, seated next to him. Inside, Esther appears again at the king's bedside, together with a scribe and two furtive figures who seem to be trying to sneak away. These scenes are ambiguous. Mordecai might be telling Esther of the plot to assassinate the king. If that is so, the background scenes probably show her warning Ahasuerus of the danger to his life, and the king, in response, passing sentence on the two chamberlains, who try to escape while a court scribe notes down the judgement. Alternatively, Mordecai might be telling Esther of Haman's plan to kill the Jews, in which case the scene in the background may be meant to show Esther approaching the king unbidden, to seek his help. Literal interpretation of this part of the painting is further complicated by the fact that the king's vengeful, pointing gesture seems directed at the figure of Haman in the centre of the painting, doomed to die. Whatever the artist's precise narrative intentions, this is essentially a painting about wickedness judged, and punished.

In the bustle and confusion of the scene, figures appear to be scurrying in all directions. Even Haman, whom Michelangelo shows nailed to a cross at the centre of the scene, is represented as a figure in hectic motion, an athlete racing towards his own death. A number of beautiful drawings survive for the agonised, twisting Haman – considered by Giorgio Vasari as the single most beautiful depiction of the human form on the entire Sistine Chapel ceiling – evidence of the sheer difficulty experienced by Michelangelo in depicting a figure in such extreme foreshortening. Later artists would emulate this dramatically telescoped perspective in order to demonstrate their virtuosity, but in Michelangelo's work it is charged with a deep expressive urgency. The foreshortening compresses and heightens the sense of Haman's pain. It also enhances the pathos of the hand with which he seems to be groping for something beyond his grasp. He stretches out as if to puncture the membrane of the illusion that constrains him. The gesture is that of one reaching out, in vain, towards the helping hand of another. He looks as though he wants to be pulled out of the shallow space of the painting that is his prison and into the freedom of the world.

In choosing to depict Haman crucified, Michelangelo departed from tradition. He may have based this innovation on a fragment of scripture, because there is a single phrase in the Book of Esther, in the Vulgate (5: 14), where the word 'crux' is used to describe the form of the scaffold – which, everywhere else in the narrative, is unambiguously described as a gallows. However, it seems more likely that Michelangelo drew his inspiration from Dante's description of Haman, crucified rather than hanged, in *The Divine Comedy*. In the *Purgatorio* section of the poem, Haman is implicitly compared to the evil thief who died beside Christ, rebelling against his torments with a mixture of pain and pride: '*Poi piovve dentro all'alta fantasia / Un crocifisso dispettoso e fiero / Nella sua vista, e cotal si moria.*' ('Then reigned within my lofty fantasy / One crucified, disdainful and ferocious / In countenance, and even thus was dying.')

But why did Dante, the poet most admired by Michelangelo, place Haman on a cross? The answer is probably because he was familiar with an ancient Jewish custom of celebrating the death of Haman and the delivery of Israel by staging a mock-crucifixion. This practice was disliked by the leaders of the Christian Church, who suspected the Jews of expressing their contempt for Christ under cover of this rite. As early as AD 408, the laws of the Theodosian codex had prohibited the Jews from 'celebrating a certain feast in which they used to express very shrewdly their secret hatred of the crucified Saviour. It was a feast in memory of the fall of their enemy Haman; for they represented him as crucified, and burned his effigy on that day with great shouting and frenzy just as if he were Christ.' Such beliefs were strengthened by a concordance of dates. The Jews celebrated the death of Haman on the second day of Passover, which also happened to be the day of Christ's crucifixion. As the art historian Edgar Wind wrote, in a detailed exploration of this web of associations, 'Owing to this Christian suspicion, the celebration of the fall of Haman, a feast in memory of the successful suppression of the first great persecution of the Jews, became a reason for innumerable new persecutions.'[13]

Michelangelo's decision to place Haman on a cross, following

Dante, carries no particular anti-Semitic intent. Rather, the symbolism of his painting revives that of the ancient Jewish ritual in which the crucified Haman is indeed seen as the enemy of the chosen people – but adding to that a layer of Christian meaning, in which Haman also becomes an anti-type of Christ. His death, which saves Israel, is given the same form as the death of Christ, which shall save mankind. Through such patternings, such symmetries and reversals, Michelangelo suggests, the will of God makes itself visible.

The Death of Haman is meaningfully counterpointed with its pair, the last of the spandrel paintings, *The Brazen Serpent*, which illustrates a story from the Old Testament long believed to prefigure Christ's death on the Cross. The juxtaposition confirms the idea that Michelangelo meant Haman's death, pictured as the crucifixion of an evil man, to be contemplated in contrast to the true Crucifixion, which delivers man from evil. The story of the brazen serpent is told in the Old Testament Book of Numbers. When the Israelites rebelled against the hardship of their life in the desert, God punished them by sending a plague of poisonous snakes into their midst. They repented of their weakness and as an act of clemency God instructed his servant Moses to set up a brass serpent on a pole. All who looked upon it would be cured. Scriptural justification for seeing this episode as a prefiguration of Christ's Crucifixion was taken from no less venerable a source than the gospel according to Saint John: 'And just as Moses lifted up the serpent in the desert, so must the Son of Man be lifted up, so that everyone who believes in him may have eternal life.' (John III: 14–15)

Michelangelo indicates the christological dimension of the story by placing the brazen serpent on a pole high up in the centre of his composition, silhouetted against the sky – just as the suffering Christ appears, raised up on Golgotha, in numerous depictions of the Crucifixion. But otherwise, as in *The Death of Haman*, this is an emphatically dark interpretation of the story. In painting the last two spandrels, it seems that Michelangelo's imagination seethed with images of rebellion, sinfulness and divine retribution. The relationships of scale, which in both works are dizzyingly odd and dreamlike, express a morbid and disenchanted view of humanity. Those who sin, those who fall into temptation, are viewed as though through a magnifying glass. Their heaving, straining bodies are massively enlarged, all the more so by contrast with the diminutive figures embodying piety and purity.

In *The Death of Haman*, Esther and Mordecai have been given the slightest of walk-on parts, seeming almost to fly off like chaff in a centrifuge from the central, dominant, agonised figure of the villain on his cross. Likewise the tumbling figures of the damned in *The Brazen Serpent* are enormous, whereas the small crowd of the virtuous looks almost as though viewed through the wrong end of a telescope. A woman kneels and prays, helped by her male companion to hold her hand out to be healed. Further back, a baby on a man's shoulder reaches towards the bronze serpent. Moses is notable by his absence. *The Brazen Serpent* is like another, more crowded version of *The Temptation and Expulsion*, with snakes and sinners multiplied. Most of all, though, it resembles a Last Judgement, with the good to the right of the brazen serpent – as they are shown on the right hand of God on the last day – and the damned tumbling away to the left. Many years later Michelangelo would paint a great fresco of *The Last Judgement*, on the wall that descends from the last two spandrels.

Pondering how best to paint a biblical plague of snakes, Michelangelo's thoughts turned inevitably to the famous classical sculpture of the *Laocoön*, the Trojan priest and his sons wrapped in the coils of serpents. *The Brazen Serpent* is a painted version of the *Laocoön* that re-imagines the same grisly death as a weird orgy. Screaming figures in luridly coloured, skintight garments writhe and tumble, forming knots and tangles of humanity bound together by the glistening coils of the serpents. The painting is full of noise as well as colour, with each face twisted into a different cry of anguish. The contours of the spandrel squeeze the struggling forms together, creating a slope against which one figure rests his legs and another cramps his muscular shoulders and back. The crowd of the damned looks as though it is being gradually sucked into the narrowest recess of the spandrel, as into a dark and claustrophobic pit.

V

The Imaginary Architecture, the Bronze Figures, the *Ignudi*

The nine histories from the Book of Genesis and the four linked spandrels, recounting tales of the salvation of Israel, are themselves just part of an even larger scheme. Below and to the side of those paintings, in a multitude of other images, the artist treated themes of prophecy and revelation, and the lives of the tribes of Israel, from the time of Abraham to that of Christ. So broad was the historical scope of the Sistine Chapel ceiling that Condivi, the artist's biographer, felt able to declare that Michelangelo had embraced 'almost all the Old Testament'.

In lesser hands, the result might have been a sprawling anthology, a chaotic outpouring of figures, stories and symbols. But Michelangelo formed a work of daunting coherence from this multiplicity of subjects. He transformed the whole of the Sistine Chapel ceiling, an area of more than 12,000 square feet, into a single creation of visual art – a polyphony of forms. He did so by weaving his paintings into a fictive architectural structure that resembles a great temple or monument, open at the top. Only the nine narrative paintings themselves exist above and outside it, floating, as it were, in patches of sky far above the viewer on the floor of the chapel. This makes them harder to see, their details more difficult to discern – but that is appropriate, because they represent the highest truths and the greatest mysteries. Michelangelo was not prone to oversights or accidents. The actual architecture of the chapel, the artist's painted architecture and his myriad painted illusions – all work perfectly together, to shape the fabric of a vision.

The structure which Michelangelo devised is both magnificent and symmetrically severe. The semicircular areas above the chapel windows, which are called lunettes, contain a host of figures collectively embodying the ancestors of Christ. From every lunette rises what is known as a spandrel or severy. These contain further depictions of the ancestors of Christ. They are similar in form to the four spandrels at the vault's corners, although they are smaller and spring to a pointed arch rather than rising in a gentle curve. Like all of the structural forms above the level of the lunettes, these arches of white marble, decorated with a motif of shells and acorns, are painted rather than real.

Between each of the spandrels along the north and south walls of the chapel, and between the two pairs of spandrels at each end, twelve gigantic figures are seated on marble thrones. These are the Old Testament prophets, accompanied by the sibyls of classical antiquity, whose visions and revelations were held to have foretold the coming of Christ. A supporting cast of putti stands beneath them, an army of plump infants – crudely painted, in several cases, by Michelangelo's assistants – holding up tablets of painted stone inscribed with the prophets' and sibyls' names. The sides of the thrones on which these mighty figures sit are formed by square columns interrupted by further supporting pairs of putti, depicted this time not in the colours of flesh and blood but as if they were figures cut from marble.

Next to these carved putti, squeezed into the spaces between the prophets' and sibyls' thrones and the tops of the spandrel arches, are pairs of nude figures painted to resemble burnished bronze statues. They strike comical and often grotesque poses, like the fools or jesters in a Renaissance court entertainment. Each pair is divided by the decorative device of a ram's skull. Some of them slump in boredom, apparently stultified by their captivity. Others seem driven to the point of insanity by their confinement. The two between Ezekiel and the Persian Sibyl sit back to back, screaming in carnivalesque rage, their windblown hair symbolising the disorder of their emotions. Each nude braces himself against the curve of the arch that contains him on one side, pushing an outstretched foot against the column of the throne that forms the other wall of his prison.

Various theories have been advanced to explain the bronze figures. Some have seen them as pagan souls trapped in limbo, others as the fallen angels who rebelled against God and were expelled from heaven. But such interpretations burden these variously ludicrous and caricatured figures with a weight of significance that they seem far too slight to carry. They resemble bronze figurines adorning the ceiling's illusionistic architecture, rather than actors with meaningful parts to play, and should therefore be seen as belonging to the innocent realm of its ornament. They are, so to speak, part of the furniture. They have sometimes been compared to gargoyles, or the babooneries that mischievously lurk in the margins of medieval illuminated manuscripts. But they seem closer in spirit to the symmetrically arranged grotesque figures found in late Roman decorative painting, examples of which were excavated in Rome itself during the artist's lifetime. Michelangelo certainly knew such images, and it is likely that he not only imitated them but intended the imitation to be noticed.

More than seventy years earlier, Leon Battista Alberti had trumpeted the achievements of the first generation of Florentine Renaissance artists and architects. In his opinion, the works of Ghiberti, Donatello, Masaccio and Brunelleschi were more than equal to those of ancient Rome. Michelangelo too was an artist in the Florentine Renaissance tradition and, as he had shown with the colossal statue of *David*, it was one of his manifest ambitions to revive and surpass the art of classical antiquity. In the Sistine Chapel he set out to do so once more, but this time in the field of painting. The fictive architecture of his scheme, decorated with classical putti and bronze nudes like classical grotesques, rises to the apex of the vault like an enormous archaeological fantasy. It is a dream of Roman grandeur, revived at the heart of Christendom.

★　　　★　　　★

Above the entablature that runs along the top of the prophets' and sibyls' thrones, perched on the pedestals supported by the carved putti, Michelangelo crowned his architectural structure with one last group of figures. These nudes, or *ignudi*, as they are called, do not merely allude to the classical past, they bring the world of antiquity back to life with such vividness that it seems to move and breathe. They are far more daring and original – and far more prominent – than the grotesque bronze nudes huddled in the cramped spaces below them. Stretching, twisting and turning in a collective display of grace and elegance, they resemble living sculptures displayed on plinths. Pope Julius II, who was himself a greedily acquisitive collector of classical sculpture, may have appreciated them as a kind of imaginary adjunct to the real museum of antiquities that he himself was assembling on the Capitoline hill.

Numerous attempts have been made to wrestle these figures into conformity with the religious scheme of the ceiling. They have been allegorised as the '*animae rationali*' of the prophets and sibyls below them – physical symbols of the seers' spiritual and intellectual strivings towards God, of their struggles for enlightenment and understanding. They have been described as wingless angels, whose function is to make the vault of the chapel synonymous with the vault of heaven. They have been seen as mysterious mediators between the worlds of heaven and earth. They have been interpreted as images of the human soul, naked before God.[14]

There is no strong historical justification for any of these Christian interpretations, although the *ignudi* do perform the ostensibly religious function of displaying ten pseudo-bronze medallions decorated with scenes from the Old Testament. Condivi refers to these, albeit briefly, as 'medallions ... which simulate metal, on which, in the manner of reverses, various subjects are depicted, all related, however, to the principal narrative'. Vasari is similarly short: 'Between them, also, they hold some medallions containing stories in relief in imitation of bronze and gold, taken from the Book of Kings.'[15] The images in question were actually taken from more than one Old Testament source, illustrating scenes as various as *Abraham and Isaac* and *The Ascension of Elijah*. All are derived from the woodcut illustrations in a popular Italian bible of 1493.[16]

It is not hard to understand why Vasari and Condivi pay such cursory attention to the medallions. These may well have been included at the suggestion of a papal theologian and were perhaps once meant to 'relate', as Condivi indicates, to the 'principal narrative'. But Michelangelo gave the images such slight prominence, painting them in a technique, similar to grisaille, which makes them all but illegible from the chapel floor, that they resemble the merest ghosts of a subtext – the half-heartedly preserved relic of a diagram of discarded meanings. What draws the eye instead is the monumental and still mysterious presence of the *ignudi*.

What *do* these figures mean? What might they express? No document has been found to confirm one or other of the various hypotheses that have been advanced about their supposed religious symbolism. The two documents that *do* exist, the biographies of Vasari and Condivi, explicitly deny the figures themselves any theological content whatsoever. Condivi simply lumps them together with the 'part which does not appertain to the narrative',[17] noting their great beauty but otherwise having little to say.

For his part, Giorgio Vasari was in no doubt about their meaning and their function – namely, that of 'upholding certain festoons of oak-leaves and acorns, placed there as the arms and device of Pope Julius, and signifying that at that time and under his government was the age of gold; for Italy was not then in the travail and misery that she has since suffered'. The *ignudi* brandish sprigs of oak and sheaves of acorns, imagery that the pope had appropriated as family emblems. (He had been Giuliano della Rovere before his election as pope, the word '*rovere*' meaning oak tree.) So there seems no good reason to doubt Vasari. The idealised, classically beautiful *ignudi* were explicitly intended as a compliment to Michelangelo's volatile patron.

Attempts to give them other, deeper meanings are contradicted by their actual appearance. The *ignudi* are decoratively varied, disposed in poses that might be occasionally energetic but are invariably devoid of emotional weight or particular significance – all the more so, when their poses are compared with those of the figures in the nine histories, whose every movement and gesture is charged with significance. The *ignudi* are vacuous, inert. There is absolutely nothing sacred or spiritual about them. They bear no resemblance to angels, who are traditionally sexless beings basking in the radiance of the Almighty. All the evidence suggests that they are indeed simply decoration, drawn from the world of pagan antiquity and designed to pay a compliment to the pope. But as such, they complicate the religious meaning of the ceiling with an assertion of worldly power.

One of the principal themes of Julius II's court rhetoric was that of the 'warrior pope' as a new Caesar Augustus, whose destiny it was to reunite and re-empower Italy – not, this time, in the name of the Roman empire, but of the universal Church. This parallelism was forced home, not only in the sermons of leading divines in Julius II's circle, such as Giles of Viterbo, but also in public festivities and celebrations. After one of his several military campaigns, in 1506–7, Julius had entered the streets of Rome in a chariot drawn by four white horses, processing through a triumphal arch inscribed for the occasion with Caesar's famous words, '*veni, vidi, vici*'.

In painting a soaring classical monument, crowned with classically inspired figures embodying the idea that Julius had indeed inaugurated a new 'age of gold', Michelangelo gave permanent form to the grandiose aspirations behind such ephemeral displays of papal triumphalism. He also staked his own claim to greatness. Like Julius, he too had come, seen and conquered. He had taken on a project as challenging as any described in Pliny the Elder's stories of the great painters and sculptors of antiquity; and he had produced a result as awe-inspiring as any of the artistic remains of the classical past. The sheer scale and daunting unity of the Sistine Chapel ceiling frescoes, their classical grandeur and magnificence, the bold originality of their forms – all these amount to a declaration of Michelangelo's unswerving confidence in his own unique gifts. The ceiling expresses a profound, reflective piety. But it also reflects an immense and unshakeable sense of pride.

VI

The Ancestors of Christ

The different levels of the ceiling imply different degrees of closeness to God. In the lowest tiers are the fourteen lunettes and eight spandrels containing the ancestors of Christ. Their arrangement has caused much confusion and prompted much unnecessarily ingenious speculation. Michelangelo's source was the opening of the New Testament Book of Matthew, in which Christ's male lineage, from Abraham to Joseph, is traced across forty-two generations in a great list of names, strung like pearls on a chain of begettings:

> Abraham begat Isaac; and Isaac begat Jacob; and Jacob begat Judas and his brethren; And Judas begat Phares and Zara of Thamar; and Phares begat Esrom; and Esrom begat Aram; And Aram begat Aminadab; and Aminadab begat Naasson; and Naasson begat Salmon ... and Eleazar begat Matthan; and Matthan begat Jacob; And Jacob begat Joseph the husband of Mary, of whom was born Jesus, who is called Christ. (Matthew I: 1–16)

The ancestors of Christ embody his physical lineage, the history of his blood, whereas the popes were held to embody the unbroken line of his spiritual legacy. Michelangelo placed the ancestors directly above the fifteenth-century portraits of the popes that line the walls of the Sistine Chapel at the level of the building's windows. In this way, he softened the transition between the earlier decorations of the chapel and his own work. The portraits of the popes are arranged in a chronological order that zigzags across the chapel's north and south walls. This is also ostensibly the arrangement that Michelangelo has chosen for his depictions of the ancestors.

In the middle of each lunette, just above the window arch, a tablet is inscribed with the names of particular ancestors of Christ. The series originally began with two lunettes high up on the west wall, directly above the altar. But Michelangelo destroyed these when he returned to the Sistine Chapel, more than twenty-five years later, to paint his monumental *Last Judgement*. So Abraham, Isaac, Jacob and Judas; Phares, Esron and Aram have all disappeared into oblivion.

In its surviving form the sequence begins on the north wall, with the lunette next to *The Death of Haman*, which carries the single name of Aminadab. It continues in the opposite lunette, on the south wall, next to *The Brazen Serpent*, inscribed with the name of Naasson. It then continues to cross back and forth across the chapel, reaching its conclusion in the two lunettes on the east wall – above the entrance – which are, in accordance with the end of the list in the Book of Matthew, inscribed with the names of Matthan and Eleazar and those of Jacob and Joseph.

The inscriptions might seem to suggest that the figures in the lunettes and spandrels should be seen as literal depictions of the individuals named in the biblical succession of Christ. But the paintings themselves make a manifest nonsense of such an approach. Whereas there are forty names in the lunette inscriptions, all of them male, Michelangelo painted over ninety figures in the lunettes and spandrels, including many women and young children. The figures are often vividly realised and occasionally verge on caricatures – such as the hunchbacked greybeard in the 'Salmon Booz Obed' lunette, who stares with comical puzzlement at the carved handle of his walking stick, which is decorated with a gurning, gargoyle version of his own face. Many of the paintings of ancestors are of distinctly pedestrian quality, which suggests that Michelangelo's assistants were allowed to paint a considerable portion of this section of the ceiling. Literal interpretation of the images is made even harder by the paintings in the small spandrels above them. These contain depictions of mothers and fathers sleeping or resting with their children and swell the cast of the ancestors yet further.

The attempt to put a name to every face is plainly futile. Yet many scholars have insisted – and continue to insist – that Michelangelo's figures must correspond exactly to the biblical list in the Book of Matthew. This has produced some distinctly perverse interpretations. One example is the final lunette, over the entrance wall, which according to its label is devoted to the subject of Jacob and Joseph. Like all these compositions, it is divided into two halves by the tablet of names. To the left there is a cowed old man huddled within the folds of his yellow cloak. He is flanked by a much younger woman, in green, who seems to be dozing, and a sturdy infant shown in profile. To the right sits another young woman, with an elaborate coiffure and a lively, flirtatious expression on her face, who is flanked by an elderly man. A child perched close to the shoulder of the man receives what appears to be a loaf of bread from another child who stands on the ground. Those seeking a one-to-one correspondence between the names and the painted ancestors are forced to find

Jacob, his wife and the infant Joseph in the figures to the left; and to find Mary, Joseph and the Christ child in the figures to the right. This fails to explain why Mary and Joseph, if it really is them, should be accompanied by not one but two children. The idea was mooted that this might be a representation of the infant John the Baptist – an explanation wrecked when the ceiling was cleaned in the 1980s, revealing that the second child is in fact not a boy, but a girl. But iconographers are nothing if not ingenious and a Plan B was swiftly formulated to deal with the awkward problem. The little girl became a female personification of the Church presenting Christ with a symbolic attribute of the Eucharist.

Such exegeses, positively yogic in their flexibility, fail to answer certain questions. Why should Michelangelo have painted Jacob as a fearful, wizened simpleton? Why depict Mary, the Mother of God, as a skittish coquette? The most likely answer is that the artist never meant the individuals in these paintings to be seen as particular figures from the Bible. Even if these figures *were* to be regarded as Mary, Joseph and Christ – executed, for the sake of plausibility, by a clumsy assistant with no sense of decorum – there are many other scenes where no amount of iconographical spadework can excavate the particular identities of the particular figures shown. The best explanation is that Michelangelo, faced with the endless succession of biblical names, treated the ancestors not as individuals but as a collective representation of the peoples of Israel before the coming of Christ. He varied the figures from scene to scene, simply to avoid tedium.

Not that he eliminated tedium altogether, because the paintings in the lunettes and spandrels are conspicuously shot through with a sense of lassitude. The figures seem oppressed by boredom, weighed down by the mundanity of lives that are going nowhere.

It has sometimes been argued that these paintings demonstrate Michelangelo's humanity, his interest in depicting the ordinary existence of ordinary people. But the truth is that he paints the daily round of merely domestic life as if it were a curse.

The female ancestors are generally busier than the men. One of them spins, another weaves and another cuts cloth. Others are absorbed in suckling their babies, while the beleaguered mother in 'Asa Josaphat Joram' seems almost smothered by a surfeit of attention-hungry children. The men are occasionally drawn into such activities, although not willingly. In 'Josias Jechonias Salathiel' a couple is shown seated back to back. The woman holds one struggling child, the man another. As the children reach out towards each other, he looks across angrily towards her – while she does her best to ignore him – as if to say that he has done more than his fair share of babysitting. Another male ancestor is writing in a rather desultory way, but most are shown slumped in attitudes of melancholic lethargy. Several of them doze fitfully, heads lolling, and one – in 'Aminadab' – sits bolt upright with an expression of exasperated impatience on his face. They have the stunned and listless air of people travelling on an underground train, or stranded at an airport, or sitting, apprehensively, in a dentist's waiting room.

Within the scheme of the ceiling as a whole, the ancestors represent a phase of human history and an aspect of the human condition decreed by divine plan. They may carry within them the physical seed of Christ but they are themselves spiritually unenlightened. They live in a time of waiting and receive no word from God, no sign or revelation. Condemned to a vacuity symbolised by the bare and shallow spaces they occupy, they are kept company only by each other, and by their shadows, cast prominently on the blank walls behind them. They are like the inhabitants of Plato's cave, who see only the dancing shadows of truth but are blind to truth itself.

Michelangelo includes more images of Christ's ancestors in the eight spandrels above the lunettes on the chapel's north and south walls. Here once more they are shown in small family groups, sitting or lying on bare ground. The compositions of these scenes strongly recall traditional representations of the Holy Family on the Flight to Egypt. Like Mary and Joseph fleeing with their child, the ancestors in the spandrels are people on the run. Many of them look exhausted and several have fallen into a deep sleep. They are shown not in rooms, like their cousins in the lunettes, but outdoors, sometimes against dark backgrounds that suggest the night sky. Some of them recline on bags or sacks, which reinforces the impression that they are refugees or fugitives. They call to mind the archetypal image of the wandering Jew, as well as embodying the biblical idea that life on earth is merely transient, an act of passing through – a journey through 'the land of the shadow of death' (Isaiah 9: 2). They are the 'strangers and pilgrims on the earth' (Hebrews 11: 13). They also evoke the words of David's blessing of the Lord (I Chronicles 29: 15): 'For we are strangers before thee, and sojourners, as were all our fathers; our days on the earth are as a shadow.'

VII

The Prophets and Sibyls

One level above the ancestors in the lunettes, and next to the ancestors in the spandrels, sit the Hebrew prophets and the sibyls of pagan antiquity. These are the largest figures on the Sistine ceiling. They were always intended to be imposing but the artist made them progressively bigger as he worked his way along the chapel. The earliest to be painted are about thirteen feet tall, the last just a few inches short of fifteen feet – well over twice the height of the average man in Rome today, and nearly three times the height of men in the time of Michelangelo. Their height is equalled by their bulk, which is further emphasised by the sculptural folds and flashing chromatic brilliance of the robes that drape them – salmon-pink, lemon-yellow, moss-green, sky-blue.

Each of the figures is a monument. Their stony draperies surge about them in frozen billows, so that they resemble a group of brightly painted monumental statues. But they also have the Pygmalion quality, of statues come to life. Their gestures and expressions are charged with emotion. They emanate a powerful psychological complexity. The curvature of the ceiling imparts a teetering quality to the perspective of the scenes at this level, so the prophets and sibyls loom over the chapel floor, seeming to project forwards precipitously from the wall. As a result, they feel closer to the real world – in both body and mind – than any of the other figures on the ceiling.

Human conduits of divine intention, the bearers of prophecy and vision, they are mediators between God and the world of man. Whereas the ancestors of Christ carry his seed, unknowingly, from generation to generation, the prophets of the Old Testament actively foretell Christ's advent. They are lightning conductors for the flash of divine revelation.

The prophets are accompanied by the sibyls, female seers of ancient times whose visions and oracular sayings were also held to have prophesied the coming of Christ. The utterances of the sibyls had first been collected by the Roman Christian author Lactantius in the early fourth century AD. The sibyls themselves had been represented in the art of the Middle Ages and the earlier

Renaissance but had never loomed as large as they do in the vault of the Sistine Chapel, where they are given equal status with the prophets. Michelangelo's innovation reflects the shifting theology of his times. In fifteenth-century Italy, humanist scholars had pioneered a revival of interest in the writings of the classical and early Christian periods, as a result of which the sibyls had become the focus of renewed attention. The culmination of this process was the publication of a treatise on *I Vaticini delle Sibille* – the oracles of the sibyls – by the Dominican friar Filippo Barbieri, in 1481. The attributes which Michelangelo gave to some of the five sibyls whom he chose to represent suggest that he, or somebody advising him, was familiar with this book.[18]

Michelangelo painted the Cumaean, Delphic, Erythraean, Persian and Libyan sibyls. Why he chose these five, from a possible ten, is not known for certain. The Cumaean Sibyl appears in Virgil's Fourth Eclogue, where she prophesies a golden age to come. This was interpreted by Christians as a veiled prophecy of the coming of Christ, given to the pagans of Greco-Roman antiquity. The Delphic, Erythraean, Persian and Libyan Sibyls – who hailed from Greece, Ionia, Asia and Africa – may have been selected to indicate the broad geographical reach of Christian prophecy within the pagan world.

To Michelangelo's more learned contemporaries, they might have contained a message for the present too, symbolising the evangelical duty of the modern Church. The Sistine Chapel ceiling was painted at the dawn of the great age of exploration, the age of Columbus and Vasco da Gama. The scope of the known world was rapidly expanding. The discovery of new continents and new races of people gave rise to the hope that Christianity would now fulfil its destiny to reach to 'the ends of the earth' (Psalms 18: 5). The sibyls had spread the message of Christ to the

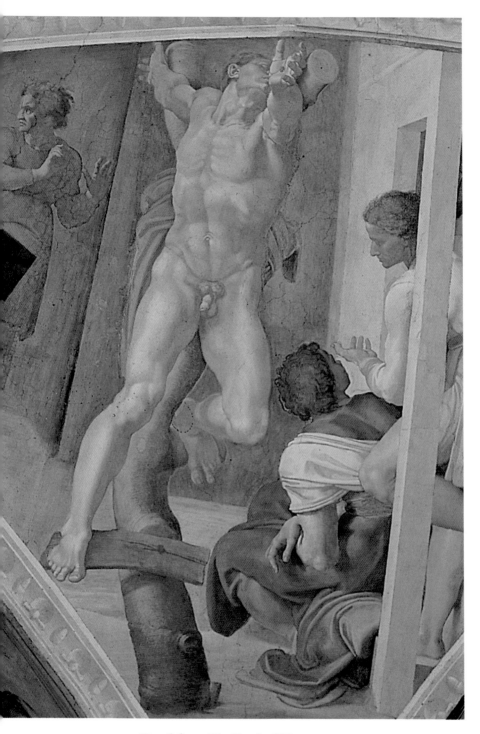

Detail from *The Death of Haman*

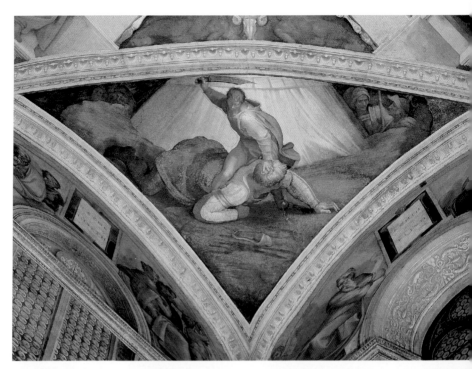

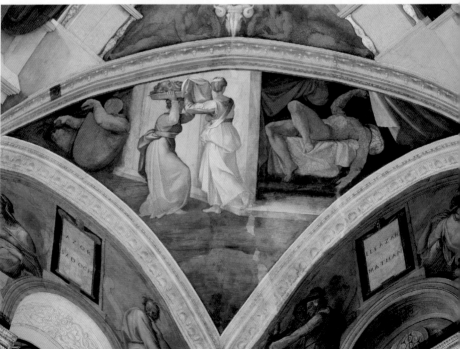

David and Goliath (above) and *Judith and Holofernes* (below)

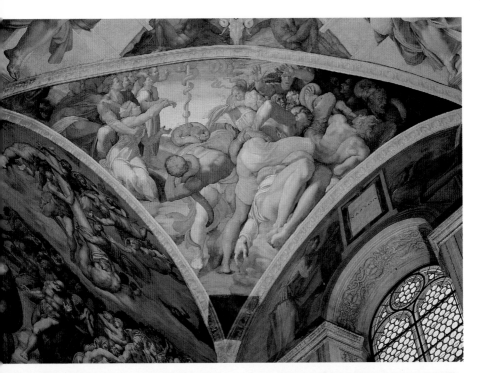

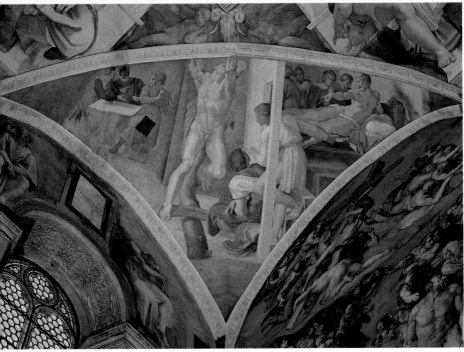

The Death of Haman (below) and
The Brazen Serpent (above and overleaf)

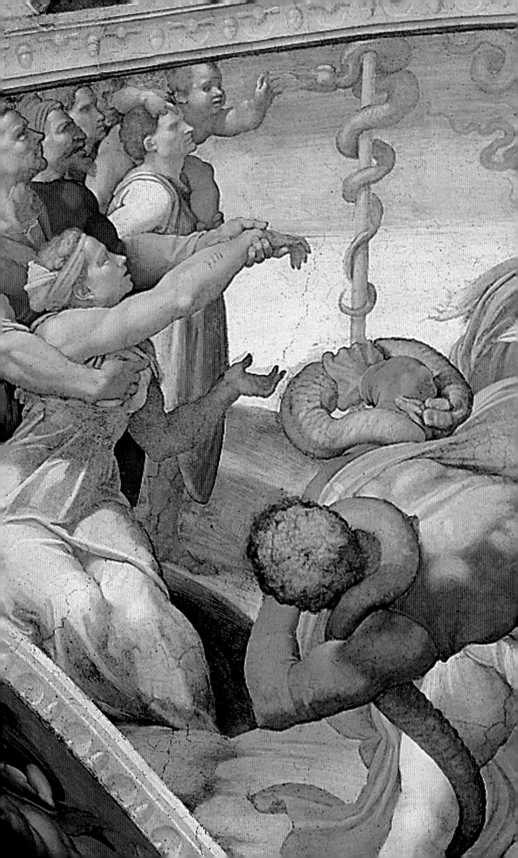

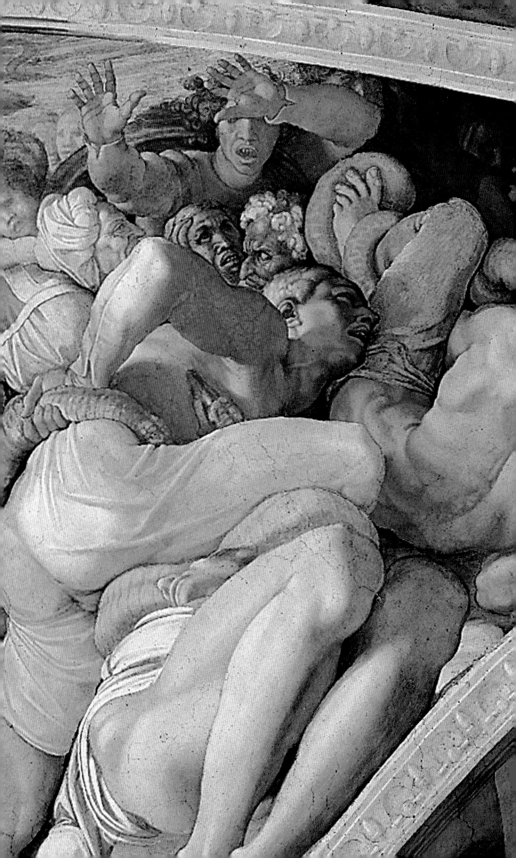

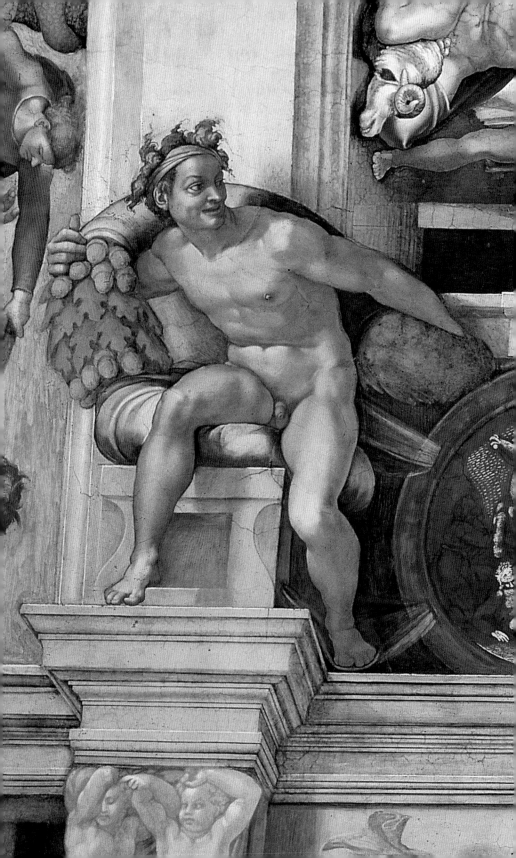

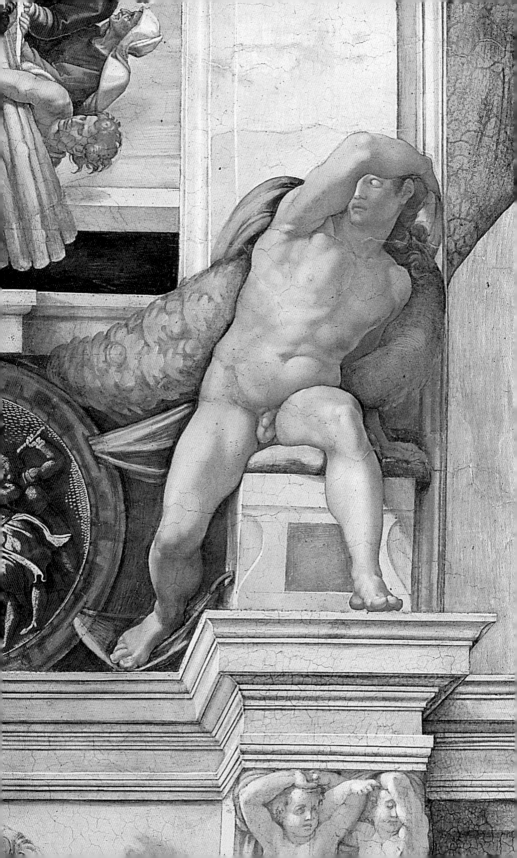

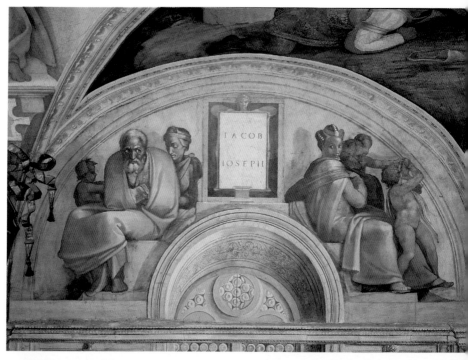

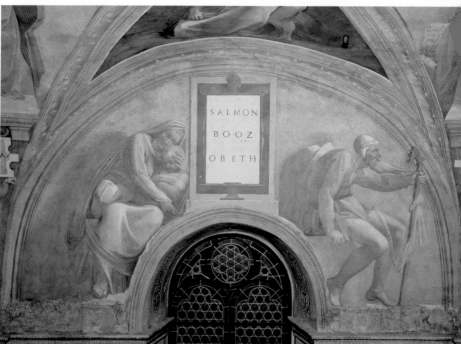

Above: two lunettes from the Ancestors of Christ sequence

Previous page: two of the *ignudi* that frame the central narratives

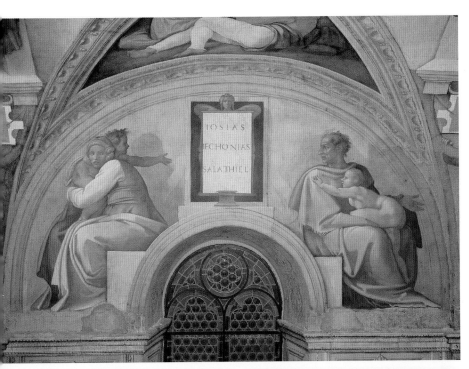

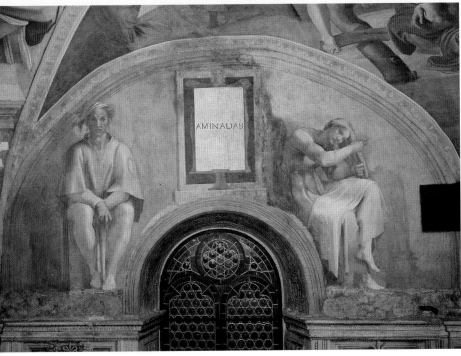

Two lunettes from the Ancestors of Christ sequence

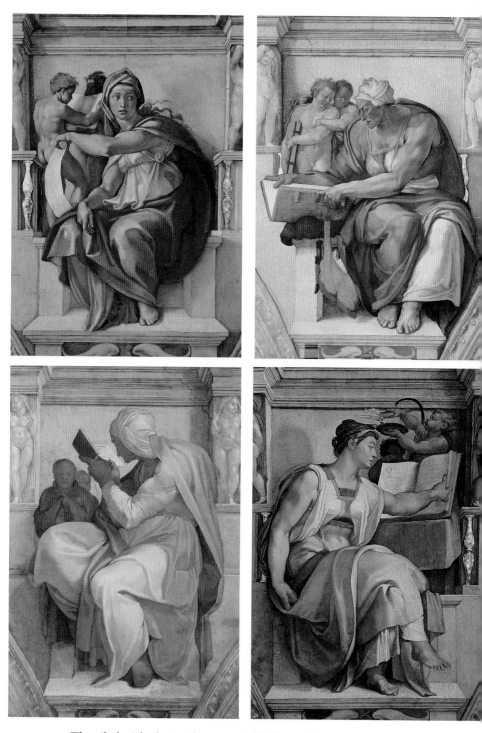

The sibyls: (clockwise from top left) *The Delphic Sibyl*, *The Cumaean Sibyl*, *The Erythraean Sibyl* and *The Persian Sibyl*

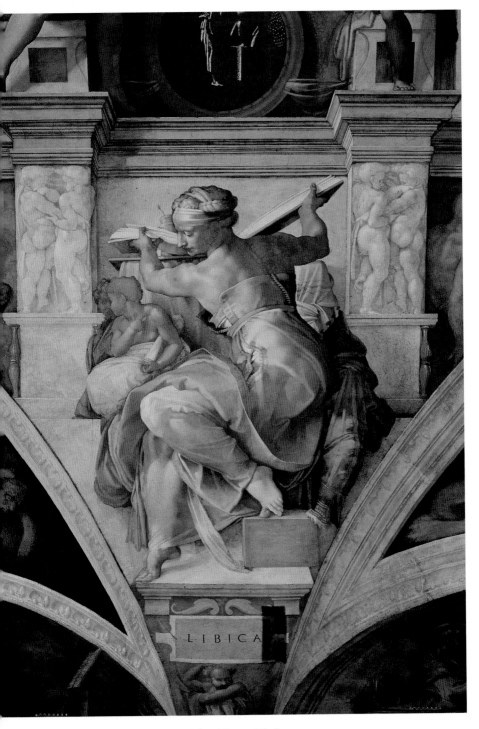

The Libyan Sibyl

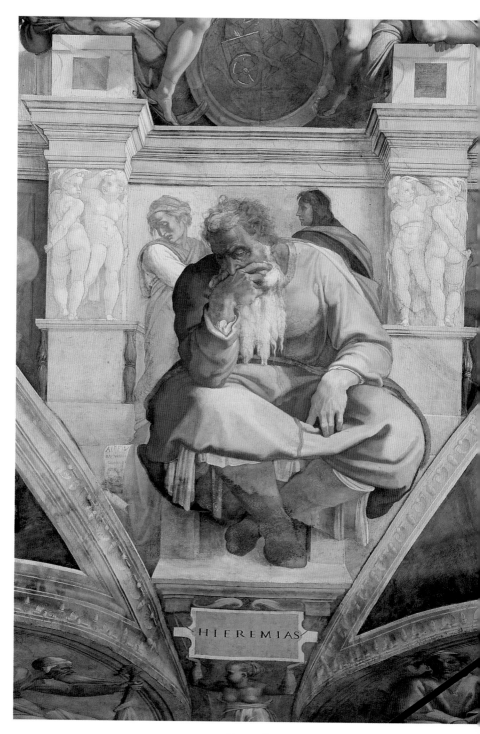

Jeremiah

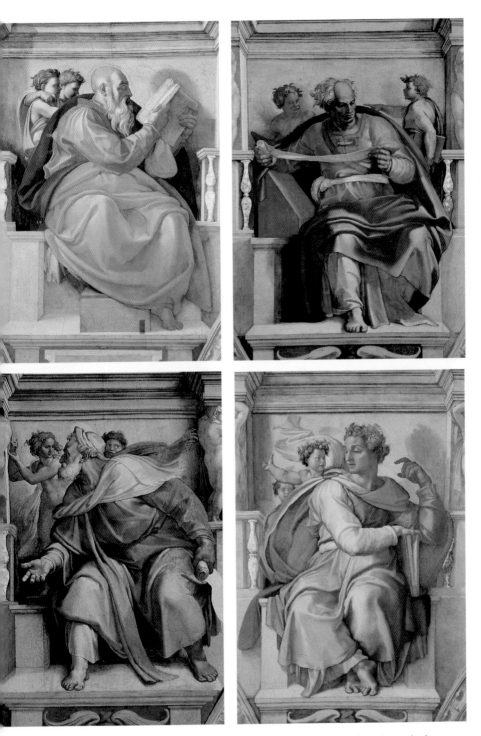

The prophets: (clockwise from top left) *Zechariah*, *Joel*, *Isaiah* and *Ezekiel*

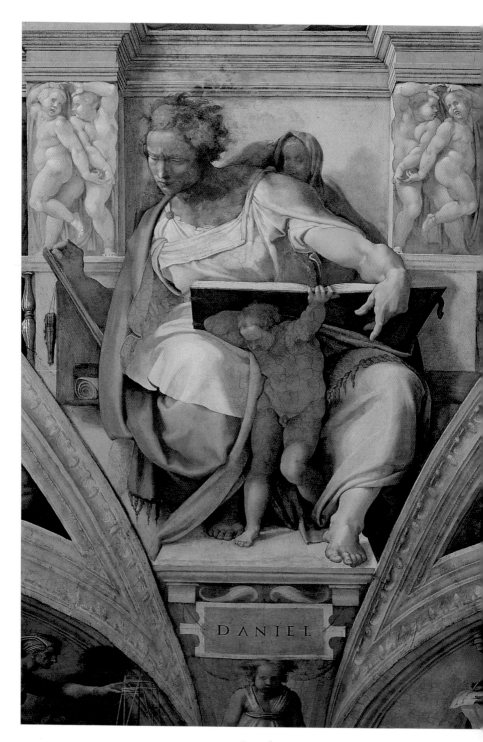

Daniel

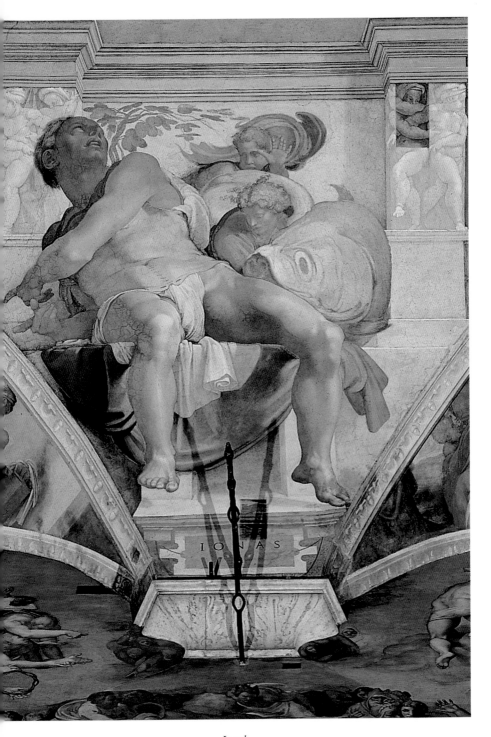

Jonah

Overleaf: a view of the Sistine Chapel interior showing
The Last Judgement

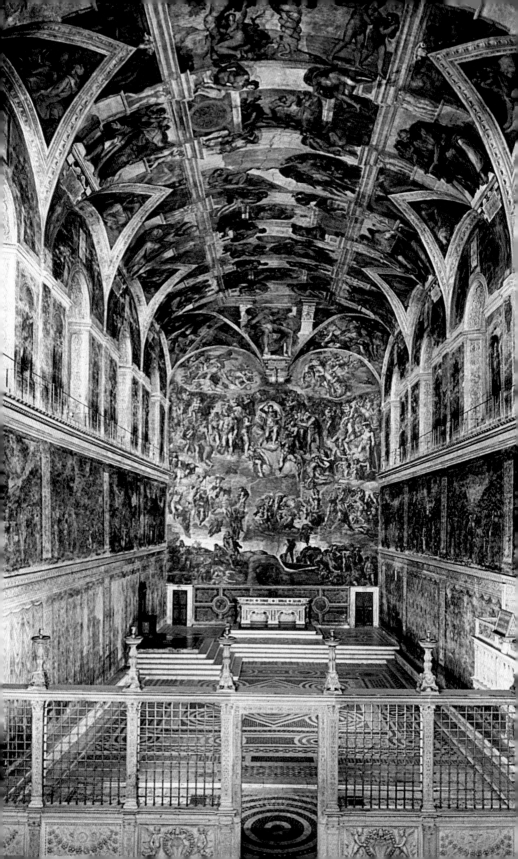

peoples of the whole world in times long past. As it was once, so must it continue to be. The presence of these figures on the ceiling anticipates the zeal that would soon dispatch Christian missionaries to the Americas, to the Pacific islands, to all corners of the world.

The act of putting the sibyls at the heart of the Vatican – a word etymologically derived from *vaticino*, meaning prophecy or oracle – was also a statement of Messianic belief. A golden age, such as that described in the visions of the Cumaean Sibyl, was also foretold by the apocalyptic preachers of early sixteenth-century Christianity – and explicitly associated by Giles of Viterbo, among other preachers close to the papacy, with the reign of the warlike Julius II. The idea of a Julian 'golden age', symbolised already on the Sistine ceiling by the figures of the *ignudi*, is given another dimension by the presence of the sibyls. In the eschatological thinking of the time, a renewal of Christian mission was to be the prelude to the last days, the Final Conflict between Christ and Anti-Christ that would herald the end of the world. So the sibyls stand not only for the universalism of the Church but for the imminence of the end of time.

This pattern of meaning is forcefully implied in the figure of *The Libyan Sibyl*, who has been placed at the end of the line of prophets and sibyls on the south wall of the chapel, directly above the altar. She is lit from below, which may have been Michelangelo's way of suggesting the light of God mystically emanating from the altar itself. In Barbieri's treatise of 1481, the Libyan Sibyl's prophecies of Christian illumination were given particular emphasis: 'Behold the day shall come, and the Lord shall lighten the thick darkness.' She twists away from the book that she holds in her two hands – a graceful gesture imbued with a sense of finality. She is closing the prophetic text, having seen the future. As she turns, she looks to her left, as if to contemplate the writhing figures, harbingers of the Last Judgement, wrapped in the coils of serpents in the spandrel of *The Brazen Serpent*. Fate and destiny have almost run their course. Judgement is nigh.

The Persian Sibyl is another figure with apocalyptic associations. In Christian theology she was held to have prophesied the beasts of the Apocalypse, heralds of the Last Judgement. Michelangelo depicted her as an old woman, poring myopically over the pages of a book that she holds so close it is almost pressed up to her face. She is shown in what is known as '*profil perdu*', turned away from the viewer to the point where her profile is so oblique it is almost lost. Her mouth is slightly open, as if she is muttering to herself the words of a prophecy she does not yet fully understand.

By contrast, *The Erythraean Sibyl* is younger and more composed. She sits relaxed, her right arm by her side while with her left she turns the pages of a book. She is accompanied by two *genii*, who resemble children or putti but are metaphorically the spirits of her inspiration. One, half asleep, drowsily rubs his eyes, while the other lights a lamp, signifying the flame of divine revelation – and perhaps indicating that moments of insight are apt to occur late at night, when the midnight oil is being burned.

The Delphic Sibyl is a figure of Grecian elegance, who turns away from the scroll she has been contemplating to gaze wide-eyed into the distance. The artist may have intended to suggest the moment just before revelation occurs. Her attention has been caught, she is aware that something is about to be disclosed to her, but she does not yet know exactly what it is.

The most sharply individuated of all the female seers is *The Cumaean Sibyl*. She is a wizened, doughty old woman, who sits hunched in concentration over a weighty tome. She is ancient in accordance with her legend, which tells that she was loved, in her youth, by the sun god Apollo. Apollo had promised her as many years of life as the grains of sand she could hold in her fist, but when she refused his advances he doomed her to age and infirmity. Her face is as leathery as parchment, her immense, sinewy arms burned by the sun. She frowns, clutching her book so earnestly that she might be trying to squeeze the meanings out of it.

The figures of the prophets are as carefully varied as those of the sibyls. *Jeremiah*, who sits opposite *The Libyan Sibyl*, is every inch the author of the Book of Lamentations, mourning the sins of the Jews and the captivity of Palestine. A brooding figure with a long and unkempt white beard, he is turned in upon himself in an attitude of unshakeable melancholy. Like some mythological giant on whom a spell has been cast, he looks as though he has been turned to ice or stone by the profundity of his own sorrowful thoughts. The long white strands of his beard resemble icicles, or stalactites. He rests the weight of his head on his great right hand – a pose that would be borrowed, centuries later, by Auguste Rodin for his celebrated sculpture *The Thinker*.

All of Michelangelo's prophets are thinkers, although *Jeremiah* is unusual in having been characterised precisely as he appears in the Old Testament. Of the others, the same can only be said of *Jonah*. As a group they seem to have been designed as generic embodiments of the gifts and burdens of prophetic thought. Their role has sometimes been compared to that of the chorus in Greek drama but they are too introverted for that. They do not comment on the story of God's plan for mankind but struggle, within themselves, to understand it.

Collectively, they dramatise an inner turbulence, a form of mental experience so extreme that it is transmitted through every nuance of gesture and expression. *Isaiah* is caught at a moment of reverie, while the bookish *Zechariah* has the air of an ancient librarian, lost in concentration. *Daniel* is depicted in the wrenching throes of intellectual struggle. As he reads from one great book, held up for him by one of his attendant *genii*, he writes furiously in another. The wild tresses of his blond hair, mysteriously wind-blown even in the solitude of his private study, crackle with the electrical energy of his thoughts. *Joel* appears puzzled by the text that he studies, holding it up close as though he is not just reading, but *rereading*, its difficult words. For his part, *Ezekiel* almost drops his scroll in distraction. One of the two *genii* accompanying him has called his attention to something unseen, something outside the painting. He starts in surprise, wheeling through space to gaze out at whatever his vision might be.

Attempts have been made to allegorise each of the prophets and sibyls as the embodiment of a sacred gift, such as Wisdom or Understanding. But each one seems too complex, too divided, to be so simplified. The sense that these figures stand for the conflicts of prophetic thought, rather than particular prophetic gifts or qualities, is enhanced by the *genii* who accompany them. These occasionally mischievous, entertaining little figures are external representations of the prophets' ideas and inspirations. They are busy, not still, and each prophet is attended by more than one of them, which itself suggests the way in which their minds are teeming.

The prophets cannot be described as masters of their own thoughts. The revelations that come to them are mystic gifts that arrive from outside, often unbidden. They are sent from heaven, by the grace of God. It is the role of the pre-Christian seers and visionaries to understand those ideas, to grasp their significance and to transmit them to the rest of mankind. But the prophets and sibyls are granted only partial revelations, glimpses and frag-ments that foreshadow the coming of Christ and the illumination of his teachings. They gain access to divine truth but the processes

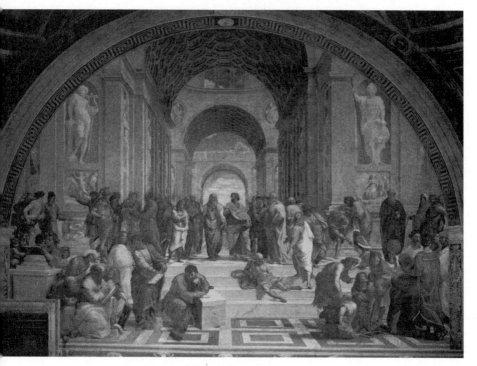

The School of Athens *by Raphael*

by which they do so are obstructed and mysterious – as mysterious as the ways of God to man. What they see, they see as through a glass, darkly.

An instructive contrast to the figures of the prophets and sibyls is to be found in the most celebrated work of Michelangelo's younger rival, Raphael: *The School of Athens*, of 1510–11 (above), exactly contemporary with the creation of the Sistine Chapel ceiling. Painted for the Stanza della Segnatura, in Pope Julius II's private apartments within the Vatican, the fresco shows an idealised representation of the progress of human knowledge. In a large and airy classical basilica, the wise men of all times are gathered. At the centre of the group, Plato points upwards to indicate the realm of Ideas, while beside him Aristotle points to the ground, to indicate his contrasting belief in the empirical basis of true knowledge. Wisdom emanates from these two figures to the crowd surrounding them on both sides, spreading in a ripple effect among the learned of all times. Man's intellectual progress is symbolised as a dynamic continuum, an extended conversation taking place across the millennia.

Only one figure seems excluded from this sociable parable of human advancement. He sits in isolated introspection, head propped on one hand, lost in his own thoughts. He is the classical philosopher Heraclitus (below). As legend would have it, he is also Raphael's portrait of the solitary and introspective Michel-

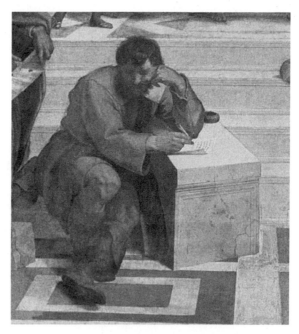

Detail from Raphael's School of Athens
showing Heraclitus

angelo. The identification is by no means certain, although the broad face does seem close to that revealed in Michelangelo's own self-portraits, with its distinctive flattened nose (the result of a fight in his youth with the sculptor Pietro Torrigiano, who punched him in the nose so hard that, in Torrigiano's own words, he felt the bone crunch 'like a biscuit'). The lonely Heraclitus is also the one figure in *The School of Athens* to have been painted in apparent imitation of Michelangelo's own style. He is more monumental than the other figures, and considerably more melancholic. His pose closely resembles that of *Jeremiah* and he might almost be one of the Sistine ceiling's prophets displaced to an alien setting. His jarring presence, in a painting to which he does not seem to belong, may well have been Raphael's sardonic commentary on Michelangelo's dour sensibility. The contrast between the two painters, one sociable and courtly, the other very much the loner, is reflected in the story that tells of their meeting one day in the Piazza San Pietro outside the Vatican. Raphael, as usual, was surrounded by a large entourage of pupils, admirers and hangers-on; Michelangelo, as usual, was on his own. 'You with your band, like a bravo,' he wryly remarked; to which Raphael shot back, 'And you alone, like the hangman.'[19]

Knowledge does not come to the seers on the Sistine vault as it comes to the crowd of easily conversing intellectuals in *The School of Athens*. Divine inspiration is nothing like the advance of secular wisdom. It comes effortfully, unpredictably – not in fluid ripples, but in spasms of revelation decreed by the mystery of divine will.

★   ★   ★

The most vividly troubled of Michelangelo's prophets is *Jonah*. Placed directly above the altar, he brings the progression of male and female seers to an uneasy climax. Condivi, who was perhaps reflecting Michelangelo's own sense of the importance of this figure within the overall scheme of the ceiling, described it in terms of breathless admiration: 'most remarkable of all is the prophet *Jonah*, situated at the head of the vault, because, contrary to the curve of the vault and by means of the play of light and shadow, the torso which is foreshortened backward is in the part nearest the eye, and the legs which project forward are in the part which is farthest. A stupendous work, and one which proclaims the magnitude of this man's knowledge, in his handling of lines, in foreshortening, and in perspective.'[20]

Condivi was struck by the skill with which Michelangelo had handled such a difficult composition. But *Jonah* is also a master-piece of characterisation. It is Michelangelo's heartfelt depiction of the prophet to whom he himself, perhaps, felt closest.

To appreciate the subtleties of the painting, it is necessary to consider the Old Testament text that inspired it. The tale is told in the four laconic chapters of the Book of Jonah. It is a parable of divine mercy and justice, in which God's goodness is thrown all the more sharply into relief by the failings of the man chosen to execute his purposes. The biblical Jonah is as Michelangelo shows him: unruly, disobedient and perpetually baffled by God's intentions.

At the beginning, God commands Jonah to go to the great city of Nineveh 'and cry against it: for their wickedness is come up before me' (Jonah 1: 2). Jonah resists, taking flight on a boat bound from the town of Joppa to Tarshish. So God sends down a storm, which so terrifies the mariners who have taken Jonah on board that they cast him into the sea. The prophet is saved from drowning by a great fish, which rises from the deep and swallows him. He spends three days and nights in its belly, praying for forgiveness, after which God orders the fish to vomit Jonah forth on dry land. Once again, Jonah is ordered to preach to the Ninevites. This time he obeys, telling the people of the city that they are doomed and that Nineveh will be overthrown within forty days. They repent of their evil ways. God takes pity on them and relents.

This displeases the irascible Jonah, who rails against God for sparing the city and making him look like a false prophet. Like a teacher confronted by a refractory schoolchild, God decides to teach him another lesson. By this time, Jonah has left Nineveh in a rage and is camping outside the city, still in the hope of seeing it destroyed. God causes a gourd vine to grow above Jonah's head, giving him shelter from the fierce sun. But the next day he sends a worm to destroy the vine. When it withers, the sun beats so strongly on Jonah that he wishes he were dead, but still he rages at the heavens. 'I do well to be angry, even unto death,' he shouts. God reproves Jonah for his sorrow over the death of a mere plant, scolding him for having felt pity over the gourd vine, but none for the people of Nineveh, 'wherein are more than six score thousand persons'. The prophet's response to this shaming lecture is not recorded because the story ends abruptly at this point. Michelangelo may have intended to paint this moment, when Jonah is struggling to absorb the contrast between his own mean-spiritedness and God's infinite mercy. His hands make a gesture associated with dialectical reckoning, with the sifting and weighing of arguments.

Jonah is the only one of the prophets and sibyls on the ceiling not to carry a book or scroll. He is shown not as scholar or thinker but as a man in action, living out the drama of his story. Michelangelo denies him the sculptural draperies of the other prophets, dressing him instead in a sea-green jerkin and a swathe of white drapery, gathered in awkward knots and folds under his arms, that also serves as a loincloth. Its dishevelled folds look half-soaked, damply clinging to the architectural ledge on which the prophet is perched. He leans backwards to stare up, wide-eyed and open-mouthed, at the heavens. He is both the cowardly mariner and the sunburned rebel. He is half-naked in the sodden clothes that he was wearing when the great fish vomited him up; his skin is red and raw.

Behind him Michelangelo has included the biblical whale, which actually looks like a giant monkfish laid out on a fish-monger's slab, and brings to mind Condivi's story about how the young Michelangelo had once painted a picture (long since lost) of Saint Anthony tormented by fish-like demons: 'he would go off to the fish market, where he observed the shape and colouring of the fins of the fish, the colour of the eyes and every other part . . .'[21] Perhaps he went to the fish market again before painting this picture.

Half-obscured by the great fish with its single, staring eye, two *genii* accompany Jonah and embody his own conflicting emotions. One is a young boy, his face framed by a swag of flying red drapery, who looks troubled and raises a hand as if pleading with God for mercy. The other is a youth with blond hair, whose eyes are cast downwards in an expression that seems to speak of shame or some other state of inward penitential reflection. From behind Jonah's left shoulder springs the gourd vine, its green leaves turning dry and yellow towards the end of its tendrils.

According to the New Testament Book of Matthew, Jonah was the clearest Old Testament archetype of Christ. Like Christ, he had been entombed, only to be resurrected: 'For as Jonah was three days and three nights in the whale's belly; so shall the Son of man be three days and three nights in the heart of the earth' (Matthew 12: 40). Because of where it has been placed the figure of *Jonah* is the very first detail of the entire ceiling to come into view of someone entering the chapel through the door in the entrance wall (an element of the original experience that has been lost by the reconfiguration of entrances and exits made necessary by mass tourism). The largest and most prominent of all the figures on the ceiling, he not only stands for Christ, but also represents a great paradox – namely that the weakest, most absurd and most impertinent of the prophets is also the one who, through his very fallibility, most clearly reveals God's infinite mercy and justice. Michelangelo must have been moved by this aspect of Jonah's story, because he lays great emphasis on it.

Whereas the other prophets and sibyls strive to know God through the word, Jonah is both stunned and blessed by a direct encounter with God himself. The artist emphasises the nakedness of Jonah's encounter. He is a being in the throes of existential revelation, thrown into a state of utter disequilibrium by his experience. His lack of fine clothing contrasts with the sculptural drapery that dignifies the figures of the other prophets, but it also works as a commentary upon their grandeur, stripping it bare to reveal the truth that lies beneath. Ultimately all must be as naked before God as he is.

Is it fanciful to detect a profound sense of fellow-feeling in the way that Michelangelo depicted the unruly and turbulent Jonah? There are striking parallels between the story of Jonah, as an unwilling instrument of God's will, and that of Michelangelo himself.

Like Jonah, Michelangelo had been instructed to preach the word of God, when Pope Julius II commissioned him to paint the Sistine Chapel ceiling. Like Jonah, he had fled from the burden of that responsibility, running away from Rome in 1506 in a rage because the pope had cancelled the monumental tomb on which he had already done so much work. And like Jonah, he was prone to moments of black despair, when he would rail at the heavens over the perceived injustice of his treatment. His poetry includes a particularly bitter sonnet dedicated to Julius II, in which the artist castigates his patron for giving credence to certain rumours – he does not specify which – that have blackened his name. As the poem reaches its disenchanted conclusion, Michelangelo's complaints to Julius metamorphose into a more general lament about the injustice of the heavens:

> At first I hoped your height would let me rise;
> The just balance and the powerful sword,
> Not echo's voice, are fitted to our want.
>
> But virtue's what the Heavens must despise,
> Setting it on the earth, seeing they would
> Give us a dry tree to pluck our fruit.[22]

The idea of a divine blessing granted only to be withheld, conveyed by the metaphor of a God-given tree that turns out to be 'dry', strongly recalls Jonah's withered gourd vine.

The prophet's awkward pose, straining backwards and bending his neck to look up to the heavens, is one that the painter himself knew well. By the time he painted *Jonah*, one of the last figures to be completed, the artist had spent much of the past three years twisted into a similarly uncomfortable position. As Giorgio Vasari recounts in his life of the artist, 'The work was executed with very great discomfort to himself, from his having to labour with his face upwards, which so impaired his sight that for a time, which was not less than several months, he was not able to read letters or look at drawings save with his head backwards.'[23] As he reels backwards, *Jonah* stares upwards at the figure of God the father on the ceiling above him. But in this too he might be a proxy for Michelangelo himself, looking up at the great expanse of the ceiling that he has painted for three years – the work that has put him through such a mixed array of emotions and that he has now, at last, finished.

PART THREE

The Last Judgement,
and Other Endings

Less than fifteen years after Michelangelo had completed the painting of the Sistine Chapel ceiling, Rome was to be devastated by one of the most traumatic events in its history. Julius II was succeeded by Leo X, who continued his predecessor's strategy of improving and aggrandising the city, and was equally happy to resort to simony and the sale of indulgences to achieve his goal. The unintended consequence of these policies was the Lutheran Reformation. Leo X was succeeded by Hadrian VI, whose brief pontificate (1522–3) was followed by that of the ineffective Clement VII (1523–34). His machinations were to bring disaster both to the papacy and to the people of Rome.

By the time of Clement's election, the Reformation had shaken Christianity to its core and Italy had been overrun by two great foreign powers, France and Spain. The world of Michelangelo's youth had been altered beyond recognition. The Italy into which the artist had been born – a place of religious certainty, economic prosperity and relative political stability, for all the ebb and flow of its petty state rivalries and mercenary alliances – was now a thing of the past. Clement VII struggled to reassert the authority of the Church of Rome while pursuing an ill-judged and badly managed strategy of constantly shifting his political alliances. He ran the risk of alienating Francis I, the French king, by giving frequent support to the ruler of Spain, the Holy Roman Emperor, Charles V. But he also infuriated Charles V with his clumsy attempts to undermine Spanish rule in the north of Italy by seeking to maintain the independence of Milan.

In the spring of 1527, Charles V's exasperation finally boiled over. The imperial armies pushed into central Italy and then on to Rome itself. They consisted of three groups. There were 6,000 Spanish *tercieros*, bent on humiliating the prince of the Church who had been bold enough to challenge their emperor. There was a ragtag troop of Italian irregulars led by hired mercenaries. Most fearsome of all, there were some 14,000 German lands-knechts, all of them rabidly anti-papal Lutherans. None had been paid for months. By the time they arrived, in early May, they had degenerated into a rabble. But they broke through Rome's feeble defences with ease and immediately set about laying waste to the city.

As Clement VII retreated to the heavily fortified Castel Sant'Angelo, churches and convents were pillaged and their contents flung into the street. Holy relics were used as target practice and sacred manuscripts torn up for horse litter. Nuns were raped and murdered. Priests were stripped naked and forced to participate in obscene parodies of the Mass. Luther's name was scratched into Raphael's fresco of the *Disputa* in the Vatican apartments (under raking light, the graffito is still visible today). A troop of landsknechts gathered beneath the pope's window and loudly threatened to eat him. On the first day alone, some 8,000 citizens of Rome lost their lives. By the end of the siege 23,000 had died, out of a total population of 53,000.[1]

Michelangelo was safe in Florence during the Sack of Rome.

In its aftermath, Clement VII belatedly made his peace with Emperor Charles V, who was himself shocked at the extent of the horror he had unleashed, an event that was soon being compared to the ancient destructions of Jerusalem, Carthage and Babylon. In penitential mood, the pope commissioned Michelangelo to paint a *Fall of the Rebel Angels*, an allegory of Promethean hubris punished by God, but the picture was never painted. During the pontificate of Clement VII's successor, Paul III (1534–49), that commission became *The Last Judgement*, an enormous fresco that was to be Michelangelo's final contribution to the decoration of the Sistine Chapel.

The pope gave Michelangelo the entire altar wall to paint, destroying an important part of the decoration of the lower part of the chapel – including Perugino's altarpiece of *The Assumption of the Virgin* – to make space for the work. The artist began *The Last Judgement* in 1535 and only finished it in 1541. There are various explanations for the delay. He had other projects in hand, having been given the unprecedented title of Chief Architect, Sculptor and Painter to the Vatican palace. In addition, the pace at which he could work had slowed with advancing age. Vasari tells the story that the artist fell from his scaffolding in the course of painting the fresco, injuring his leg so badly that he was reduced to 'a desperate state'.[2] His wounds were tended by 'an ingenious physician' from Florence, and the artist was eventually able to return to work. But time had taken its toll. Twenty-seven years had passed since he had accepted the commission to paint the vault of the Sistine Chapel. He was sixty-one years old when he started *The Last Judgement* and sixty-seven when he completed it. Michelangelo was no longer a young man.

★   ★   ★

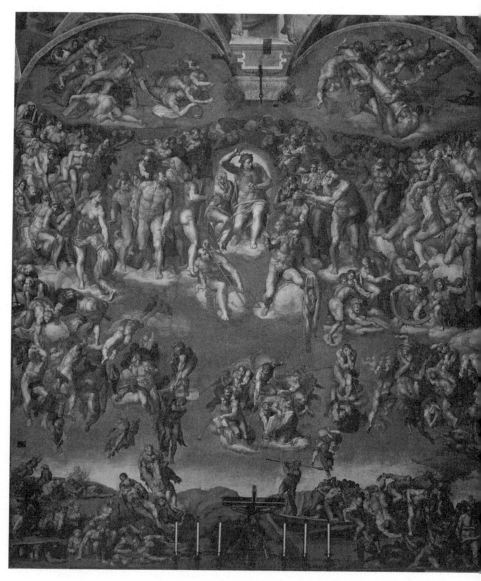

The Last Judgement

It was traditional to depict Christ on the Last Day seated on a throne like a judge, but the artist ignored precedent and looked directly to the Gospel of Matthew:

> Immediately after the tribulation of those days shall the sun be darkened, and the moon shall not give her light, and the stars shall fall from heaven, and the powers of the heavens shall be shaken: And then shall appear the sign of the Son of man in heaven: and then shall all the tribes of the earth mourn, and they shall see the Son of man coming in the clouds of heaven with power and great glory. And he shall send his angels with a great sound of a trumpet, and they shall gather together his elect from the four winds, from one end of heaven to the other.
> (Matthew 24: 29–31)

The figure of Michelangelo's Christ appears in the centre of a dark blue sky, the vault of heaven. He is beardless, in a striking departure from Italian Renaissance convention. This apparent innovation seems to have disconcerted one or two churchmen among Michelangelo's contemporaries, but there was a venerable precedent for it. The artists of early Christian Rome and Byzantium had represented Christ without a beard, making him resemble earlier, classical representations of the youthful sun god, Apollo. Perhaps Michelangelo was inspired to revert to that ancient archetype by Matthew's reference to the darkening of the sun. His Christ too resembles Apollo, whose powers are incorporated in his omnipotence. Supported on a cloud, he blocks out the light of the sun so that its rays halo him with light.

The gestures with which he separates the good from the evil are forbiddingly solemn. His left or sinister arm is turned against the damned, whom he consigns to an eternity of torment in the fires of hell, the mouth of which beckons far below. With his

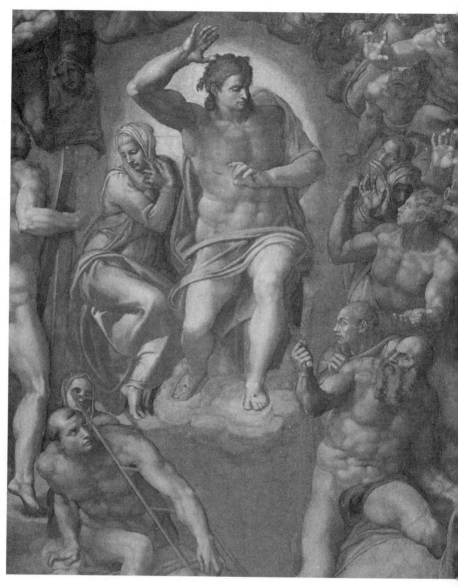

The vengeful figure of Christ from The Last Judgement

raised right arm, he summons the blessed to heaven, although Michelangelo makes even this act of apparent benediction look punitively severe. The hand that blesses might also be poised to strike. Christ looks down to his left, which indicates that his thoughts are absorbed by those who have sinned. He is the embodiment of retributive anger. The saints gathered around him, who include the wizened St Peter holding a pair of massive keys, and St Bartholomew clutching the flayed skin of his own martyrdom, seem daunted and awestruck rather than joyful. Even the Virgin Mary, seated beside her son, cowers and looks away.

Below the vengeful figure of Christ, angels sound the last trump to awaken the dead. Michelangelo has arranged this group so that it resembles a kind of bouquet of figures from which long and spike-like trumpets protrude like thorns. The artist's source, here, was not the gospel of Matthew but the Book of Revelation. Condivi points this out in his biography of Michelangelo, adding a revealing gloss on the other figures in this group, who hold up a great book and peer into its pages: 'In the central part of the air, near the earth, are the seven angels described by St John in the Apocalypse ... Amongst these are two other angels holding an open book in which everyone reads and recognises his past life, so that he must almost be his own judge.'[3] The idea that each man must ultimately pass judgement on himself was surely Michelangelo's own. It is typical of the sombre, self-reflective thoughts that preoccupied him in his later years.

To Christ's left, the lower part of the painting is crammed with writhing and tormented figures. The air is choked with a throng of entangled nudes, a wriggling crowd that recalls the snake-entwined multitude of *The Brazen Serpent*, which Michelangelo had painted many years earlier on the ceiling of the chapel. Below,

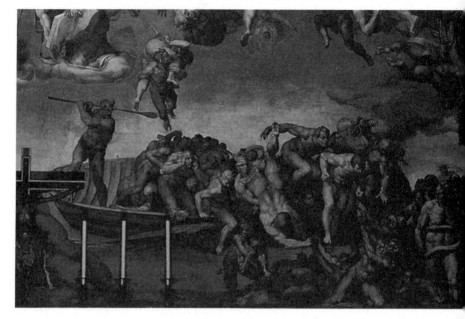

Detail from The Last Judgement, *showing Minos, bottom right*

in a detail drawn from Dante's *Inferno*, Charon delivers a boatload of the despairing damned into the clutches of devils. This too calls to mind one of the scenes on the ceiling, being a convulsive variation on the theme of doomed figures in a boat, which had first appeared in *The Deluge*. As if to emphasise such echoes, Michelangelo has even twined a serpent around Minos, the judge of the underworld, who appears in the bottom right-hand corner of the painting. The figure grimaces as the snake bites his genitals.

According to Vasari, Minos is the only portrait in *The Last Judgement*.[4] The figure was apparently Michelangelo's revenge on Pope Paul III's master of ceremonies, a man named Biagio da Cesena, who had dared to protest that the artist was violating the sanctity of the chapel with painted obscenities – a complaint, presumably, about the picture's large cast of nudes and many scenes of violence. Vasari also says that when Biagio complained to the pope about the portrait, the pontiff merely shrugged his shoulders and declared that it was beyond even his power to release anyone from hell.

To Christ's right, the dead struggle from the ground with what seems like a weary reluctance to be reborn. Some of these figures remain buried to their waists in the ground, while others have emerged as skeletons waiting to be clothed in the flesh of their resurrection.[5] Angels wrestle with demons to drag and hoist the blessed up towards their salvation. But the overwhelming impression is one of arduous, precarious struggle. The whole composition is overbearingly top-heavy, so that even the teetering pile of nudes scrambling heavenwards looks as though it might at any moment come crashing down to earth. The figures whirled round in the vortex of the painting have none of the grace and beauty of the newly created Adam or the soaring airborne God on the chapel's ceiling. They are heavy, lumpen beings, formed from a coarser mould. Even the Apollonian Christ is comparatively ungainly, his torso broadened to such an extent that it has become nearly square.

The Last Judgement is an uneasy and unwelcoming work of art, a vision of salvation and damnation so crowded that there is no room left in it for anyone else. Its disturbed, tumultuous structure makes the possibility of anyone being truly saved seem almost hopelessly remote. Legend has it that when Pope Paul III saw this troubled dream of a picture for the first time, he instantly fell to his knees and uttered a prayer: 'Lord, do not charge me with my sins when you come on the day of Judgement.'[6]

★   ★   ★

Michelangelo in 1541 was no longer the exuberant prodigy, full of plans for the tomb of Julius II, who had once dreamed of carving a colossus out of a mountain to amaze passing seafarers. *The Last Judgement*, with its crowded, awkward forms, is a renunciation of beauty that also contains within it the artist's repudiation of his own youthful pride – the hubris that had led him to believe he could carve from stone, or paint with coloured earth, forms so grand and vivid they might rival those shaped by the hand of God.

The Lutheran Reformation had exerted a profound influence on Michelangelo, as it had on so many others within the Roman intelligentsia. Like every conscientious Christian believer of his time, he had been forced into an awareness not only of the corruption of the Roman Church, but of the extent to which it had lost touch with much of the essence of Christianity itself. Many effects of the Reformation may have been unwelcome and destructive, but there is no question that Catholics everywhere, and especially in Italy, were profoundly impressed by the ideas emanating from Protestant Germany – particularly the idea of every man's duty to form his own direct relationship with God, the idea of the universal priesthood, and the doctrine of justification by faith.

In the 1530s, Michelangelo had begun a passionate friendship with a widowed noblewoman named Vittoria Colonna, who was a leading figure in the nascent Catholic reform movement in Rome. Together, they listened to readings from the Epistles of St Paul, and meditated on Christ's sacrifice. Michelangelo gave a number of drawings of *The Crucifixion* to Vittoria Colonna to assist her in such contemplation, works of such heightened feeling and piety that they seem to predict the art of the Baroque. Through her he was also introduced to the Spanish preacher Juan de Valdés, a leader of the Roman reform movement, who was influenced

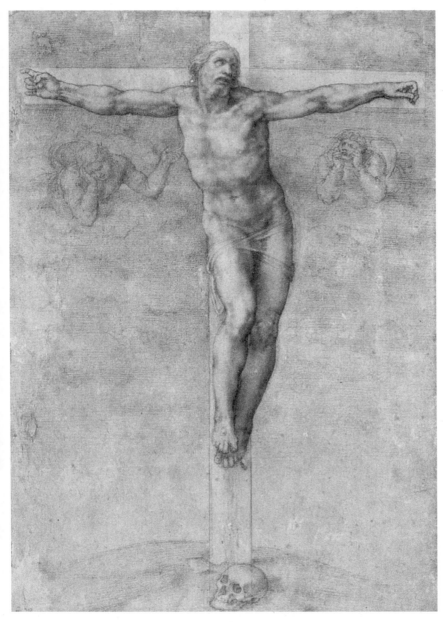

One of the drawings of The Crucifixion *given to Vittoria Colonna*

by the teachings of Erasmus and who preached the doctrine of the justification through faith alone. Michelangelo, who called

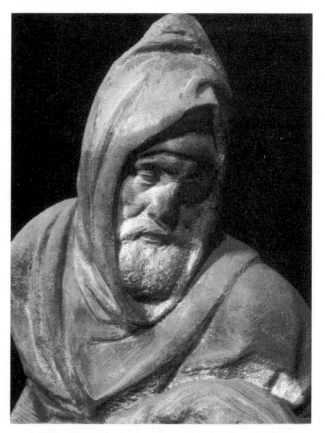

Michelangelo as Nicodemus in The Florence Pietà

faith 'the gift of gifts', had much earlier in life been influenced by the severe piety of Savonarola, who had also preached the importance of faith and called vigorously for the reform of the Church. So he may have felt that the religious rebirth of his later years had been marked out for him since his youth.

In painting *The Last Judgement*, Michelangelo embarked on a new course in his art, which henceforth was to be characterised by a harsh asceticism and a deeply felt sense of spiritual urgency. The phases of his late style mark the different stages of a progressive withdrawal from the world. His two monumental frescoes for the Pauline Chapel of the Vatican, *The Conversion of St Paul* and *The Crucifixion of St Peter*, painted in the mid-1540s, renounce the grace of the Sistine Chapel ceiling even more decisively than *The Last Judgement*.[7] In sculpture, he created *The Florence Pietà* in the early 1550s, a work in which he included his own self-portrait, as Nicodemus, helping the Virgin Mary to bear the weight of her dead son. From 1555 to 1564, the year of his death, he worked obsessively on the block of stone that was to become known as *The Rondanini Pietà*, a sculpture so inchoate and harshly emotional that it resembles an unfinished work of the Middle Ages.[8]

The spirit of renunciation and humility implicit in Michelangelo's later work is the subject of Giuliano Sacco's poem about the artist, written in Latin (which was the language of the Church in Michelangelo's time):

Pingo sculpo scribo	*I paint, sculpt, write,*
Perspicio imitor	*I transcribe my intuitions,*
Nihil creo	*I create nothing,*
Deus tantum creat	*God alone creates.*
Homo creatur sacrum	*Man is created sacred,*
Carnis spiritusque conubium	*Union of flesh and spirit.*
Deus est creat amat	*God is, creates, loves.*
Labe originali incumbente	*Fruit of original sin,*
Inter bonum malumque	*Between good and evil*
Deus ponit hominem	*Man is sustained by God,*
Sed manum Suam	*Who holds out his merciful hand*
Misericordem tenet	

Proximam manui	*Close, very close, to the hand*
Imaginis Suae	*Held out by his own image.*
Alter ad alterum	*One toward the other,*
Uterque tendit index	*Two index fingers point and stretch,*
Usque ad tactum	*Reaching for the contact that will come*
In aeternae vitae splendore	*Only in the splendour of eternal life.*
Tensio autem	*This tension is no equipoise.*
Eadem non est	
Homo petit Deus dat	*Man searches, God gives.*
Haec voluntas Dei	*This is the will of God*
Sic sors hominis	*And that is the destiny of man.*
Hoc humanae genti	*This is what, to mankind,*
Ostendere volo	*I want to signify*
Per ipsam artem	*Through the art*
Quam mihi donat	*Given to me*
Pulcherrimus Deus[9]	*By most beautiful God.*

The very last drawings that Michelangelo ever touched are shot through with a profound tremulous humility. Each shows Christ suffering on the Cross, with the Virgin and St John agonising over his miseries. They have a strange and ghostly quality. The faces are smudged and the forms seem to struggle into recognisability, each one haloed by a multitude of lines, showing that Michelangelo – who kept them and worked on them for many years – went over them repeatedly with his pencil and with his fingers. They are less like drawings than repeated prayers, every line like a bead told on the rosary. They preserve the artist's attempts to bring the dying Christ before his eyes, to feel his presence and comprehend the mystery of the divine made flesh – and to do so, obsessively, time and time again, as he felt his own death approaching. They call to mind one of his last recorded statements, made while pacing the streets of Rome in the rain one day in 1564: 'I can find peace nowhere.' Looking at them feels almost like a form of trespass, like eavesdropping on 'the divine Michelangelo' at the moment when he felt least divine, and most human – the moment when he was readying himself to meet his maker.

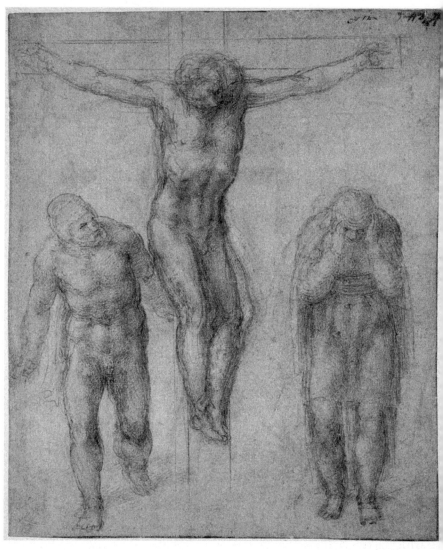

The Crucifixion with two mourners, one of Michelangelo's last drawings

CONCLUSION

T he brooding presence of *The Last Judgement* on the altar wall of the Sistine Chapel inevitably complicates the experience of looking at the ceiling above. The work casts a long shadow. It projects the penitential sense of spiritual mission that Michelangelo developed in later life on to the frescoes that he had painted while still a young man. Turning from *The Last Judgement* to the Sistine Chapel ceiling, the viewer is apt to pay greater attention to the more severe and apocalyptic elements of the earlier frescoes – to find in scenes such as *The Deluge*, with its helpless throng of the doomed, or *The Brazen Serpent*, with its tumble of agonised bodies, vivid foreshadowings of Michelangelo's later, darker, vision. The paintings of the Sistine Chapel ceiling certainly express a severe and deeply pious Christian conception of the pattern of universal history, and of mankind's place within it. But *The Last Judgement* is liable to make that conception, that vision, seem rather more bleak than it was originally intended to be.

The fact that Michelangelo himself reshaped the meanings of his own great fresco cycle in later life raises larger questions of interpretation. How do the ceiling's many images relate to one another? In what order or hierarchy should they be viewed? What is the nature of the plan according to which those images are arranged, and what exactly is the vision that underlies it? Was the plan Michelangelo's own, or was he painting to a theological programme devised by others? If he *did* receive instructions, to what extent did he follow them, and to what extent did he exercise creative licence? These issues are fiercely debated in the existing literature about the Sistine ceiling.

No documentary evidence has been found to settle such questions. But it seems improbable that Michelangelo was allowed total freedom in his choice of scenes and subjects for such an important commission. It is likely that he discussed his ideas, that he sought advice and that he needed approval of some kind before going ahead with the actual painting. But a number of scholars go considerably further than that modest set of assumptions. They argue that Michelangelo must have worked to a specific and theologically demanding programme – a document, perhaps augmented by a diagram, which not only dictated the subject matter of every one of the images on the ceiling, but also composed them into a pattern of cross-references and allusions designed to convey a particular set of complex and arcane theological propositions.

Such scholars have gone to great lengths to reconstruct that hypothetical document, to identify its author and explain the ways in which his theology shaped Michelangelo's frescoes. The leading theologian of Julius II's pontificate, Giles of Viterbo, has often been proposed as the author of such a text. One author has suggested that Giles wrote a complex programme based on the venerable theology of St Augustine's *City of God*, and that concealed within Michelangelo's frescoes there lies an allegory of Augustine's two cities, the earthly and the heavenly. A forcefully argued counter-suggestion also has Giles as the author of the programme, but asserts that his source of inspiration lay not in St Augustine but in the writings of a twelfth-century Franciscan mystic named Joachim of Fiore, whose writings were the focus of renewed interest in early sixteenth-century Rome. Other candidates proposed for the authorship of a programme for the ceiling include another papal theologian by the name of Marco Vigerio, as well as Cardinal Alidosi – with whom Michelangelo agreed the contract to paint the ceiling – and a disciple of Savonarola's by the name of Sante Pagnini. Each solution is different, but all are inspired by the same dream, that of finding a single code or key to unlock the totality of meaning embodied in the pictures.

Theologically totalitarian interpretations of the ceiling all have major flaws. This is not only because they are marred by numerous demonstrable failures of fit with the actual paintings of the chapel (as critics of each hypothesis have been swift to point out). It is because they all represent what in philosophy might be termed a 'category mistake' – a fundamental error about the very nature of that which they seek to describe. There is little point in debating the respective merits of different attempts to find a key to the Sistine ceiling, precisely because it is the very idea of a complete explanation, in the form of an underlying text that might magically explain all, that is itself at fault. There is no good reason to suppose that Michelangelo was ever required to paint in accordance with an all-encompassing programme. It was not common practice to devise such programmes. No such text has been found for the Sistine Chapel ceiling, despite years of archival research undertaken in the hope of finding such a thing. In fact no equivalent document, nor any reference to one, has been found for any major fresco cycle, painted anywhere in Italy, at any time during the Renaissance. So while it is reasonable to assume that Michelangelo discussed his ideas with people whose opinions he respected, it is highly unlikely that he allowed himself to be enslaved by any single, rigid theological framework.

★   ★   ★

It is well worth remembering that the *visual* structure of the Sistine Chapel ceiling – namely, the monumental imaginary architecture that contains all of its imagery – also plays a vital part in determining how that imagery is seen and felt and understood. It dictates the scale relationships of the various parts – making, say, the prophets and sibyls loom large and the ancestors seem less important. Such discrepancies of scale are integral to the semantics of the ceiling. They ensure that the figure of Jonah, for example, is much more prominent – more significant, more *meaningful* – than that of any of the figures below him. Moreover, it seems certain that the imaginary architectural fabric, which plays such a crucial role both in the arrangement of the images and in the shaping of their meaning, was a structure Michelangelo himself both invented and insisted on. It is, as stated earlier, a painted version of the tomb for Julius II, which the artist had been planning for years. It was a form that he passionately wanted to create, whether in sculpture or painting. In the absence of evidence to the contrary, it must be assumed that he chose it for the ceiling – and that he found most of the solutions that made it work.

It is clear from looking at the pictures themselves, which owe so little to the traditions of medieval and Renaissance art, and so much to the naked words of scripture itself, that Michelangelo read and reread the Old Testament continually while he was painting the Sistine Chapel ceiling. Condivi pointedly reports the fact in his biography, so it can be assumed that Michelangelo wanted it to be known. Between them, the biographies of Condivi and Vasari reveal a great deal about how Michelangelo wanted posterity to judge his achievements in the Sistine Chapel. Some of this information takes the form of direct assertion. Vasari's story about Michelangelo locking all his assistants out of the chapel makes it fairly clear that the artist wanted to be seen as the sole author of the work. Admittedly, it is not a story that has much bearing on the question of whether he was given theological guidance – but Michelangelo had already answered that question with his letter to a friend, written in 1523, in which he recalled telling the pope that his first idea for the ceiling was a 'poor thing', and Julius II replying that Michelangelo could do whatever he wanted.

The texts of the artist's biographers contain numerous stories that obliquely touch on questions of authorship and originality. Vasari says that Michelangelo 'would not allow any of his works to be seen' until they were finished and that he even resorted to violence to escape supervision – and, by implication, potential meddling. 'On one occasion,' writes Vasari, 'when the pope had bribed his assistants to admit him to see the chapel ... Michelangelo, having waited in hiding because he suspected the treachery of his assistants, threw planks down at the pope when he entered the chapel, not considering who he might be, and drove him forth in a fury.'[1]

Several other stories carry the same essential thrust of meaning – asserting in essence that Michelangelo knew what he wanted to create, that he was the best judge of what was appropriate, and that ultimately he would not brook interference from anyone with the temerity to think they knew better. This is the moral of the story of Piero Soderini, who dared to criticise the nose of the *David* and was then fooled by the artist into accepting the work without alteration. It is also the moral of another of Vasari's stories about the Sistine Chapel, according to which the pope – showing an old-fashioned taste for gold and glitter – foolishly asked Michelangelo to add touches of gilding to the ceiling after it was finished in order to give it a more splendid effect. Vasari recounts that Michelangelo dissuaded him from such vulgarity by saying, 'Holy father, in those times men did not bedeck themselves with gold ...' The ceiling, Michelangelo's ceiling, remained as it was.

One of the most revealing stories in Condivi's biography does not directly concern the Sistine Chapel ceiling – although it surely has a bearing on it – but relates to the statue of the *Pietà* that he had created several years earlier. Condivi recalls a conversation with the artist in which the subject of the Virgin's unusually young appearance, in that work, had come up; and he recorded the artist's own explanation of it:

> ... there are some who object to the mother as being too young in relation to the Son. When I was discussing this one day with Michelangelo, he answered: 'Don't you know that women who are chaste remain much fresher than those who are not? How much more so a virgin who was never touched by even the slightest lascivious desire which might alter her body? Indeed, I will go further and say that this freshness and flowering of youth, apart from being preserved in her in this natural way, may also conceivably have been given divine assistance in order to prove to the world the virginity and perpetual purity of the mother.'

What is really striking about the story is that it presents Michelangelo thinking out loud about the ways in which art can express the subtleties of meaning implicit in the story of Christ's incarnation, God's manifestation in the body of a man. He thinks as a theologian might think, and asks himself theological questions. How would Mary have looked? What form would God have given her, to express his purposes? He plainly regards himself as independently equipped – and entitled – to find those answers within himself, within his own intuitions. Condivi was sufficiently struck by the remarks to make his own comment on Michelangelo's unusual grasp of such matters: 'This consideration would be most worthy of any theologian and perhaps extraordinary coming from others, but not from him whom God and nature formed not only to do unique work with his hands but also be a worthy recipient of the most sublime concepts.'[2] One of the most fascinating aspects of the whole passage is the way in which it conveys Michelangelo's sense that it is entirely appropriate for him to rethink a particular religious theme, to treat it afresh, rather than to rely on established authorities and conventions.

Many authors have chosen to disbelieve Michelangelo's insistence that he was allowed to do whatever he liked in the Sistine Chapel. But while he may have exaggerated his freedom, the balance of probabilities suggests that he did indeed take the licence to reinvent and reconceive the meaning of the stories from the Old Testament that were his subject, filtering and refracting them through the lens of his own intellect, his own reading, his own sensibility. That is not to say that he was given no advice, and neither is it to say that he did not on occasion modify what he painted on the basis of that advice. But Michelangelo insisted so often and in so many ways on his own ultimate autonomy – in his correspondence, in the stories that he fed to his biographers – that it would seem peculiarly patronising to question the essential truth of what he so clearly attempted to communicate. He was a pious man and a brilliant painter. The chances are that he was indeed trusted to paint the ceiling as he liked once his basic themes had been established and approved.

★   ★   ★

The fundamental assumption behind the interpretation of the Sistine Chapel ceiling offered in this book is that Michelangelo felt that he was sufficient of a theologian – as Condivi's story indicates – to paint his own vision of what he believed to be the eternal truths of Christianity. That vision is full of subtleties and complexities and will continue to be the subject of debate and argument – one of the hallmarks of any great work of art being its ability to inspire passionate disagreement among those who care about it. But ultimately, what makes Michelangelo's vision so powerful is its combination of monumentality and directness.

To approach the Sistine Chapel ceiling as if it were an icono-graphical picture puzzle, to go to it in quest of secret meanings and veiled correspondences, seems fundamentally perverse – like going to the music of Bach, not to be moved, but to hunt out the mathematical principles that might underlie its harmonies. The essential meanings of the cycle are unfolded across each of its levels with a great and at times chilling clarity.

The figures of the ancestors collectively embody the idea that those who exist in the absence of divine revelation are foredoomed to lives of unenlightened, unrelieved mundanity. They are the lowest of the images on the ceiling, because they represent the lowest of its several spheres of human experience.

Placed aptly above the figures of the ancestors are ranged the mighty figures of the prophets and sibyls. They incarnate the belief that the search for revelation, for direct contact with God and for an understanding of his plans and purposes, is at once the noblest and the most difficult of all human undertakings.

The nine narratives that span the vault of the ceiling, forming the apex of its meanings, tell the ancient story of Man's alienation from a God whose perfection and omnipotence will always haunt him – and which, one day, he hopes to find again. Below them, the four pendentives show the severity of God's justice and the immensity of his mercy and grace.

The nine paintings from the Book of Genesis tell a progressive story of loss and fragmentation. That story reaches its climax with *The Deluge* and might even be said to extend beyond it, reaching into the world of everyday life that lies outside and beyond the chapel itself. This effect of Michelangelo's frescoes is inseparable from the ineluctable choreography of every visit to the Sistine Chapel – which ends, inevitably and always, with the act of leaving. This might seem obvious. To experience the paintings in any building, we have to enter it. To go back to the business of our lives, we have to leave. But Michelangelo's paintings incorporate those acts into the pattern of their meaning.

Standing at the entrance to the chapel, the viewer looks up towards the altar, above which are the scenes of God creating the world, and Man. Following the course of the narrative, the viewer sees next the Fall of Man and its consequences for humanity. Looking up at the last of the nine scenes, *The Deluge*, he or she is confronted with Michelangelo's most explicit image of the fallen and sinful nature of humanity. It is under that image that all must pass, on the way out of the building. Having been drawn in, drawn up and into a vision of God Almighty, perfect and all-powerful, we are expelled, thrust back into mere mortal existence, by the momentum of the narrative.[3]

Michelangelo's fresco cycle pursues those who look at it, even as they depart from it. In leaving the chapel and re-entering the ordinary world, the visitor encounters the yet greater fragmentation – a fragmentation beyond even that of the scattered bodies strewn across the painter's *Deluge* – of the broken images that succeed one another in the course of every daily existence. Re-entering the world outside the chapel, we encounter the images that finally complete this part of its meaning. Leaving behind God in his perfection, holding in our mind's eye the mere memory or after-image of his likeness, we ourselves re-enact the destiny of Adam and Eve – which is to leave paradise, to enter the fallen world that it is the destiny of all mankind to endure.

NOTES

INTRODUCTION, *pp. 1–8*

1 Linda Murray, *Michelangelo, His Life, Work and Times*, London 1984, p. 57
2 Ross King, *Michelangelo and the Pope's Ceiling*, London 2002, p. 212
3 Murray, *Michelangelo*, p. 66
4 Andrew Graham-Dixon, *Renaissance*, London 1999, p. 201
5 Sir Joshua Reynolds, *Discourses on Art*, ed. Robert R. Wark, New Haven 1975, pp. 278–82
6 Murray, *Michelangelo*, p. 9
7 The best-known examples are Irving Stone's novel *The Agony and the Ecstasy*, which was subsequently made into a film starring Charlton Heston as the variously agonised and ecstatic artist.
8 Ascanio Condivi, *The Life of Michelangelo*, trans. Alice Sedgwick Wohl, Pennsylvania 1999, p. 58

PART ONE
Michelangelo Buonarroti and His World, pp. 9–66

1 Condivi, *Life*, p. 10
2 Giorgio Vasari, *Lives of the Painters, Sculptors and Architects*, trans. Gaston du C. de Vere, ed. David Ekserdjian, London 1996, II, p. 643

3 Condivi, *Life*, p. 9

4 Murray, *Michelangelo*, p. 9

5 Quoted in Robert S. Liebert, *Michelangelo, A Psychoanalytic Study of His Life and Images*, Yale 1983, p. 35

6 Vasari, *Lives*, II, pp. 646–7

7 James Fenton, *Leonardo's Nephew: Essays on Art and Artists*, London 1998, p. 38, remarks: 'It must have been a bit like a garden, a bit like a stonemason's yard and a bit like a school – but a school where members of the ruling elite dropped in to observe the pupils at their studies.'

8 Condivi, *Life*, p. 12

9 Condivi, *Life*, p. 12

10 Condivi, *Life*, pp. 12–13

11 Vasari, *Lives*, II, p. 649

12 Vasari, *Lives*, II, p. 649

13 Vasari, *Lives*, II, p. 649

14 Condivi, *Life*, p. 15

15 Condivi, *Life*, p. 17

16 Condivi, *Life*, p. 18

17 Eamon Duffy, *Saints and Sinners: A History of the Popes*, London 1997, p. 151

18 George L. Hersey, *High Renaissance Art in St Peter's and the Vatican: An Interpretive Guide*, Chicago 1993, p. 12

19 Damian Thompson, *The End of Time: Faith and Fear in the Shadow of the Millennium*, London 1996, p. 76

20 Hersey, *High Renaissance Art*, p. 12

21 The sculpture, now lost, is believed to have been owned by Cesare Borgia and Isabella d'Este, and then the dukes of Mantua, before passing into the collection of King Charles I of England. It was probably destroyed in the fire at Whitehall Palace in 1698.

22 Condivi, *Life*, pp. 21–3; it has also been suggested that this work was commissioned by Cardinal Riario, who refused it on the grounds of indecency, and that it was only then purchased by Galli.

23 Vasari, *Lives*, II, p. 651

24 Michelangelo, *Complete Poems and Selected Letters*, trans. Creighton Gilbert, ed. Robert N. Linscott, Princeton 1980, poem no. 18, pp. 11–12

25 The remark, reputedly made by Michelangelo to a priest whom he knew in Rome, is quoted in Michelangelo, *Complete Poems*, p. xxxv

26 Vasari, *Lives*, II, pp. 653–4

27 Vasari, *Lives*, II, p. 655

28 Vasari, *Lives*, II, pp. 654–5

29 Murray, *Michelangelo*, p. 22

30 Murray, *Michelangelo*, p. 22

31 Duffy, *Saints and Sinners*, p. 147

32 Loren Partridge, *The Renaissance in Rome*, London 1996, p. 19

33 Duffy, *Saints and Sinners*, p. 139

34 André Chastel, in *The Sack of Rome*, Princeton 1983, p. 78, notes that Giles of Viterbo passionately argued the case for continuing the sale of indulgences to Julius II's successor, Leo X.

35 Lauro Martines, in *Power and Imagination*, London 1980, pp. 416–17, argues that it was Julius II's uncle, Sixtus IV, who set the course for the division of Christian Europe. The point can be debated, but the broader thesis – that the *style* of the papacy was a direct cause of the Reformation and its discontents – is powerfully argued by the author: 'With the pontificate of Sixtus IV (1471–84), the Renaissance papacy went over to sanguinary nepotism, worldly splendour and power politics in a manner that was to contaminate the whole hierarchy of the Church in Italy for nearly a century. The glaring disparities between doctrine and conduct, between responsibility and the neglect of parishes, generated confusion and dismay, and if the Protestant Reformation was one of the consequences in parts of Northern Europe, the fragmented outcome for Italy was in mysticism, prudent silence, tiny pockets of fervent reform, extremes of cynicism and hypocrisy, and finally in the backlash of the Inquisition and Counter Reformation.'

36 Graham-Dixon, *Renaissance*, p. 205

37 Condivi, *Life*, pp. 33–4

38 Condivi, *Life*, pp. 29–30. Condivi adds that Michelangelo was inspired by 'the wish to emulate the ancients'. According to legend, Dinocrates, a Greek architect of the fourth century BC, planned to carve Mount Athos into the likeness of a human figure.

39 Condivi, *Life*, p. 30

40 Murray, *Michelangelo*, p. 52

41 Condivi, *Life*, p. 35

42 Murray, *Michelangelo*, p. 55

43 Condivi, *Life*, p. 38

44 See John Shearman, 'The Chapel of Sixtus IV', in André Chastel et al., *The Sistine Chapel: Michelangelo Rediscovered*, London 1986, pp. 23–4

45 A fascinating account of the papal conclaves and the superstitions surrounding them is given by D. S. Chambers in a brief essay: 'Papal Conclaves and Prophetic Mystery in the Sistine Chapel', *JWCI*, 41 (1978), pp. 322–6

46 James Hall, *Michelangelo and the Reinvention of the Human Body*, London 2005, p. 107

47 Sydney Freedberg puts it well in *Painting in Italy 1500–1600*, London 1970, p. 36: 'the conception and the making of the Sistine Chapel in the Vatican, which followed on the first design for the tomb and which Michelangelo was compelled to undertake instead of it, was affected essentially by his thinking for the tomb design ... that design was not abandoned with the suspended project for the tomb, it became the basis from which Michelangelo evolved his design for the vast fresco, transposing the major elements from one to the other, as if the scheme intended for the tomb should be unfolded flat upon the ceiling space.'

48 Michelangelo, *Poems*, pp. 5–6

PART TWO
The Sistine Chapel Ceiling, pp. 67–157

1 See Charles Seymour, ed., *Michelangelo: The Sistine Chapel Ceiling*, London 1972, p. 83

2 According to Giorgio Vasari, 'Michelangelo complained at times that on account of the haste that the Pope imposed on him he was not able to finish it in his own fashion, as he would have liked; for his Holiness was always asking him importunately when he would finish it. On one occasion, among others, he replied, "It will be finished when I shall have satisfied myself in the matter of art." "But it is our pleasure," answered the Pope, "that you should satisfy us in our desire to have it done quickly"; and he added, finally, that if Michelangelo did not finish the work quickly he would have him thrown down from the scaffolding.' (Vasari, *Lives*, II, p. 668) Both Vasari and Condivi tell of the Pope becoming so infuriated with the artist, another time, that he actually hit him with a stick. In Condivi's account, 'when the Pope demanded when he would finish the chapel, Michelangelo answered in his usual way, "When I can." The Pope, who was precipitate by nature, struck him with a staff which he had in his hand, saying, "When I can, when I can."' (Condivi, *Life*, p. 59)

3 See Murray, *Michelangelo*, pp. 6–7

4 See Seymour, *Sistine Chapel Ceiling*, pp. 93–5

5 Condivi, *Life*, p. 42

6 John Milton, *Paradise Lost*, ed. Alastair Fowler, London 1971, p. 496n

7 Quoted in Kenneth Clark, *The Nude*, London 1976

8 Vasari, *Lives*, II, p. 746

9 Condivi, *Life*, p. 105

10 Eugène Delacroix, *The Journal of Eugène Delacroix*, Oxford 1951, p. 181

11 See Erich Auerbach, *Mimesis: The Representation of Reality in Western Literature*, Princeton 1968

12 Charles de Tolnay, *The Sistine Ceiling*, II, London 1945, p. 45

13 See Edgar Wind, 'The Crucifixion of Haman', *Journal of the Warburg Institute*, I, no. 3 (January 1938), pp. 245–8

14 See, for example, Charles de Tolnay, *Michelangelo*, New York 1945–60, II, p. 64; Clark, *The Nude*, pp. 198–9; Seymour, *Sistine Chapel Ceiling*, passim.

15 Condivi, *Life*, p. 48; Vasari, *Lives*, II, p. 670

16 See Partridge, *The Renaissance in Rome*, p. 89

17 Condivi, *Life*, p. 48

18 See Loren Partridge, *Michelangelo, The Sistine Chapel Ceiling, Rome*, London 1996. This is a particularly helpful guide to the iconography of the ceiling.

19 Quoted in King, *Michelangelo and the Pope's Ceiling*, p. 171

20 Condivi, *Life*, p. 48

21 Condivi, *Life*, p. 9

22 Michelangelo, *Complete Poems*, p. 6

23 Vasari, *Lives* II, p. 669

PART THREE
The Last Judgement, *and Other Endings, pp. 159–75*

1 Duffy, *Saints and Sinners*, pp. 158–9; Hersey, *High Renaissance Art*, p. 27; Christopher Hibbert, *The House of Medici, Its Rise and Fall*, New York 1975, p. 245

2 Vasari, *Lives*, II, p. 292

3 Condivi, *Life*, p. 84

4 Vasari, *Lives*, II, p. 692. The frequently told story that Michelangelo gave his own features to the flayed skin held by Saint Bartholomew is a myth. None of the painter's contemporaries refer to it as a self-portrait. If it really had been a likeness of Michelangelo they might have been expected both to notice and to comment on the fact.

5 These details are closely derived from Luca Signorelli's fresco of *The Resurrection* in Orvieto Cathedral, a work which Michelangelo knew well. The apocalyptic theme and urgent, animated style of Signorelli's work seem to have exerted a powerful and lifelong influence on Michelangelo, although – perhaps characteristically – he chose never to mention it.

6 Quoted in Anthony Hughes, *Michelangelo*, London 1997, p. 254

7 For an extended discussion of these pictures, see chapter 4 of my book on the Renaissance: *Renaissance*, pp. 213–17

8 *The Rondanini Pietà* provoked Kenneth Clark to write one of his most penetrating remarks about the artist's late style: 'in the humility of his last years, Michelangelo has pared away everything which could suggest the pride of the body, till he has reached the huddled roots of a Gothic wood carving.' Clark, *The Nude*, p. 249

9 Although the poem is directly inspired by the ceiling, hence the allusions to the almost touching fingers of God and Adam, it seems to me to evoke the sombre piety of Michelangelo in his later years. It is printed here for the first time.

CONCLUSION, *pp. 177–86*

1 Vasari, *Lives*, II, pp. 662–3
2 Condivi, *Life*, p. 27
3 This aspect of the experience of the chapel has been altered by the rearrangement of entrances and exits to accommodate the vast number of tourists visiting every day. The pope and his entourage would not have experienced it in the way that I describe – they entered and left the chapel from the side – but the laity would have done so. In any case, although we no longer perform the same choreography in paying a visit to the chapel, the experience is fundamentally the same. We enter and we leave, and in leaving we are reabsorbed into the continuum of fallen, human time – taking up and re-enacting the story told in the chapel, so to speak, at the point where it leaves off.

BIBLIOGRAPHY

An extensive bibliography of the literature published on Michelangelo in the English language is contained in William Wallace, ed., *Michelangelo: Selected Scholarship in English*, New York 1996 (be warned, it runs to five volumes). There are also good specialised bibliographies to be found at the end of each of the entries on different aspects of Michelangelo in *The Dictionary of Art*, London 1996, pp. 431–61.

What follows here is a list of the sources directly referred to in the endnotes.

Auerbach, Erich, *Mimesis: The Representation of Reality in Western Literature*, Princeton 1968

Chambers, D. S., 'Papal Conclaves and Prophetic Mystery in the Sistine Chapel', *Journal of the Warburg and Courtauld Institutes*, 41 (1978) pp. 322–6

Chastel, André, *The Sack of Rome*, Princeton 1983

Chastel, André, et al., *The Sistine Chapel: Michelangelo Rediscovered*, London 1986

Clark, Lord Kenneth, *The Nude*, London 1976

Condivi, Ascanio, *The Life of Michelangelo*, trans. Alice Sedgwick Wohl, ed. Hellmut Wohl, Pennsylvania 1999

Delacroix, Eugène, *The Journal of Eugène Delacroix*, ed. Hubert Wellington, Oxford 1980

Duffy, Eamon, *Saints and Sinners: A History of the Popes*, London 1997

Fenton, James, *Leonardo's Nephew: Essays on Art and Artists*, London 1998

Freedberg, Sydney Joseph, *Painting in Italy 1500–1600*, London 1970

Graham-Dixon, Andrew, *Renaissance*, London 1999

Hall, James, *Michelangelo and the Reinvention of the Human Body*, London 2005

Hersey, George L., *High Renaissance Art in St Peter's and the Vatican: An Interpretive Guide*, Chicago 1993

Hibbert, Christopher, *The House of Medici, Its Rise and Fall*, New York 1975

Hughes, Anthony, *Michelangelo*, London 1997

King, Ross, *Michelangelo and the Pope's Ceiling*, London 2002

Liebert, Robert S., MD, *Michelangelo, A Psychoanalytic Study of His Life and Images*, Yale 1983

Martines, Lauro, *Power and Imagination*, London 1980

Michelangelo, *Complete Poems and Selected Letters*, trans. Creighton Gilbert, ed. Robert N. Linscott, Princeton 1980

Milton, John, *Paradise Lost*, ed. Alastair Fowler, London 1971

Murray, Linda, *Michelangelo, His Life, Work and Times*, London 1984

Partridge, Loren, *The Renaissance in Rome*, London 1996

Partridge, Loren, *Michelangelo, The Sistine Chapel Ceiling, Rome*, New York 1997

Reynolds, Sir Joshua, *Discourses on Art*, ed. Robert R. Wark, New Haven 1975

Seymour, Charles, ed., *Michelangelo: The Sistine Chapel Ceiling*, London 1972

Thompson, Damian, *The End of Time: Faith and Fear in the Shadow of the Millennium*, London 1996

Tolnay, Charles de, *Michelangelo*, vols 1 and 2, Princeton 1943, 1945

Vasari, Giorgio, *Lives of the Painters, Sculptors and Architects*, trans. Gaston du C. de Vere, with an introduction and notes by David Ekserdjian, London 1996, 2 vols

Wind, Edgar, 'The Crucifixion of Haman', in *Journal of the Warburg Institute*, I, no. 3 (January 1938), pp. 245–8

ILLUSTRATION
ACKNOWLEDGEMENTS

All colour illustrations of the Sistine Chapel ceiling are reproduced with permission of the Vatican Museums and Galleries, Vatican City.

PART ONE

Michelangelo Buonarroti and His World

p. ii   Autograph sonnet with self-portrait (Scala, Florence)

p. 13   Self-portrait of Michelangelo, black chalk, pricked, the Teyler Museum, Haarlem

p. 24   *The Battle of the Centaurs*, marble, Casa Buonarroti, Florence (Bridgeman Art Library)

p. 32   *The Drunkenness of Bacchus*, 1496–7, marble, Museo Nazionale del Bargello, Florence (Bridgeman Art Library)

p. 36   *Pietà*, marble, St Peter's, Vatican (Alinari)

p. 40   *David*, 1501–4, marble, Galleria dell'Accademia, Florence (Bridgeman Art Library)

p. 43   Seated male nude, *c.* 1511, red chalk heightened with lead white, the Teyler Museum, Haarlem

p. 44   Studies for Haman, 1511–12, red chalk, British Museum, London

p. 46   *The Battle of Cascina*, after Michelangelo, 1542, oil on panel, Collection of the Earl of Leicester, Holkham Hall, Norfolk (Bridgeman Art Library)

Illustration Acknowledgements

PART TWO
The Sistine Chapel Ceiling

PART THREE
The Last Judgement, *and Other Endings*

INDEX